TANDEM

Reincarnation

What do we really mean when we talk of
Reincarnation? That in some past life you, as a
person, have lived as an Egyptian pharaoh,
Roman centurion, French Revolutionary? That you,
with your twentieth-century memory, can look
back on and remember your rebirths? This is a
dream that many of us have, an experience we
long to undergo. But the author of this fascinating
book makes it clear that we are wrong. The real
truth is far more mysterious, far grander.

It is our true inner selves, our innate characters,
which reflect those past lives, and it is through
spiritual and metaphysical disciplines that we can
be aided in recollecting them.

The cover illustration
is by Richard Stanley

Reincarnation

Hans Stefan Santesson

TANDEM
14 Gloucester Road, London SW7

Published in the United States of America by
Universal Publishing & Distributing Corporation, 1969
First published in Great Britain by
Universal-Tandem Publishing Co Ltd, 1970

Copyright © 1969 by Universal Publishing &
Distributing Corporation

Made and printed in Great Britain by
The Garden City Press Ltd, Letchworth, Herts

For
Astrid and Tore

CONTENTS

REINCARNATION

Introduction

Belief in Reincarnation is a part of the history of the race. This race.

Thousands of years ago man first began to search for an explanation of why he was on this earth, how he had come, and to where he would, in time, depart.

The resulting Mystery Schools, not to be confused with the self-styled Mystery Schools of the present day, taught a series of disciplines that aided the student in the search for understanding.

The teachers, the opinions of their contemporaries to the contrary, were often very human, possessed both of the weakness and of the innate strength which gives us reason to accept the concept of multiple supra-physicals discussed in the following pages.

What I have attempted to do in this admittedly preliminary study has been to trace this belief in Reincarnation back through time. I have wanted you to listen to the Buddhists and to the Neo-Platonists, to the Christians and to the Iconoclasts, who at varying times have arrived at similar conclusions.

In attempting this I have perhaps not been as facile as is usually demanded in popular approaches to subjects such as these. I am afraid I have no apologies, for I think you will agree with me that if you are at all a serious student, or for that matter a beginning student, of metaphysics, you need to know that not only are you not alone but that you are a part of history.

You will find at the conclusion a number of books listed

that I have found particularly helpful. I must at this time express my indebtedness to Joseph Head and S.L. Cranston's extraordinary anthology, REINCARNATION, which I confess I have drawn upon frequently, almost shamelessly. I have a suspicion they will not mind, however. Like myself, they obviously believe that you need to know The Truth.

HANS STEFAN SANTESSON
New York, N.Y. 1969

I

WHAT IS REINCARNATION?

We are going to be concerned in this book with the possibility that ours is a two-fold nature—that the outer or physical "you" exists for one short cycle of perhaps sixty or seventy years, storing up a series of experience patterns during that period, while the inner "you," an indefinable but almost certainly an etheric *something* which cannot be touched, weighed or felt, but which has none-the-less been known for thousands of years, is in a sense a larger embodiment representing in its totality a pattern of several hundred incarnations throughout which that inner "you," that person within the body, in time attains a special kind of maturity.

Reincarnation poses a very special challenge. The perpetuation of a particular career over a period of time is almost impossible. The memory of the life experience will be there, hidden away in the inner recesses of what you know as the mind, and may be drawn upon, assuming you know how to do so, but dated learning or skills belong to this life or to a particular life and to its problems. Even if you have mastered a skill for which there is a special demand at this particular point in what we are pleased to call the history of the race, there is no reason to believe that this skill will still be needed in the Days After Tomorrow. The skill may be superfluous —as indeed you may be.

As a matter of fact, what you have been, or who you have been, is less important than *how* you have been it! If you have schemed your way to the top, and stepped on friends and enemies with a bland (or less than bland) impartiality, concerned only in getting up there among the elect, you will, your administrative skills notwithstanding, have to do penance for this in a later life.

No. You will not necessarily be reborn in the body of a beast of prey, or a scavenger, or any of the creatures you were no doubt called, behind your back, in your former life.

But you will be punished. Or more precisely the inner "you," the soul, will be punished. If you were a Buddhist you would know that you would chained on the wheel of life for an almost limitless time. You would be born and you would die, you would be born and you would die, you would be born again and you would die again, until you would at long last begin to undo the damage you had done, not to the physical "you," but to the spiritual inner "you."

No. I am not contradicting myself. When I said that the perpetuation of a particular career over a period of time, and I did mean Time, is almost impossible, I meant that while you may carry a memory of one life with you over to your next life, you do not get a second chance and the opportunity to undo in your next life what you did in the life just concluded, nor for that matter are you able to carry on as before.

A Napoleon is not going to be reborn as a Napoleon, a Goebbels is not going to be reborn as a Goebbels, a Stalin is not going to be reborn as a Stalin, and a shoemaker is not necessarily going to be reborn as a shoemaker. It isn't that simple!

Assuming for the sake of argument that the Buddhist concept of the transmigration of souls is valid, you may indeed be reborn as something that is the antithesis of what you were in your former life. The man who has lived and died— and no doubt laughed and loved and occasionally sinned and occasionally also been capable of grace throughout his life —literally ceases to exist. He is absorbed back into his own spiritual causal nature, which is not him, nor does it know him, but which is an all-pervading supra-physical life. He will never reincarnate again as himself, nor will his characteristics and traits be perpetuated. The universe will never again know of him.

After a period of inaction, however, the spiritual causal nature which had given him being will in a sense create a new personality. This personality will neither remember the personality that it was in its former life, nor associate its present life with that of its former life, but at the same time certain qualities will be manifested in the new personality which could not have come into expression had they not passed through certain definite stages while in the earlier personality.

In other words, the incarnating individuality of one incarnation never incarnates again. Thus while the Self, or that which animates the inner "you," can be said to give birth to an infinite number of personalities, it is this Self—not the personalities—that endures. It is not this Self that actually incarnates or Reincarnates, but from itself, from within itself, it can be said that it individualizes incarnating organisms.

As you read further, you will find that the Emperor Julian believed his soul to have manifested in a former life as Alexander the Great, and that Proclus declared that his rational nature had achieved its dignity while in the body of Nicomachus, the Pythagorean. It should be noted that they did not believe themselves to have been some other person in a former life, but rather that the rational principle dwelling in them had previously dwelt in other forms.

Plotinus wrote that it was a universally admitted belief that the soul committed sins, expiated them, underwent punishment in the invisible world, and passed into new bodies. Plato affirmed that when the soul failed to achieve liberation and willfully followed perversity, it would pass into the body of a woman, a statement which is generally interpreted to signify that the soul takes up its residence in the matrix awaiting rebirth.

The six realms of transmigration in Buddhism are: the world of the gods, the world of the demons, the realm of the hungry ghosts, the lower states of life, the animal world, and the world of human beings.

The Pythagorean doctrine of transmigration, which we shall discuss later in this book, as taught by Empedocles, was held to contain an arcane rather than a literal meaning. While apparently accepting the doctrine of the transmigration of human souls into the bodies of animals, Plotinus, about whom we shall also read later on, is considered to have possessed a knowledge of the esoteric interpretation of the doctrine because of the fact that nowhere else in his writings, or in such as are known, is he quite as ironic as when discussing the doctrine. (There is also of course the possibility that he simply could not conceive, intellectually rather than spiritually, of being reborn into the body of an animal.)

Proclus, Chalcidius, and Hermes all maintained that it was unphilosophic (!) to affirm that the human soul could ever return in the body of an animal, for the very will of the gods forever preserved so noble a creature as the soul from such a disgrace! Proclus, setting for himself the task of interpreting Plato's allusions to the return of man in a brutish constitution of form, reminded the reader that when in the *Republic* Plato declares that the soul of Thersites assumed the life of an ape, the word *life,* and not body, was very explicitly used, thus signifying that the reborn soul assumed the attitude but not necessarily the physical form of an ape. Similarly, Plato had described in the *Phaedrus* the descent of souls into a brutish life, but he did not suggest that they assumed brutish bodies, for in Platonic philosophy life is not synonymous with form. Proclus attempted to show that Plato referred solely to what might be termed the invisible constitution, and how a man living a bestial life can cause his inner nature to assume the appearance of a beast and thus be known to the wise not according to his physical body but according to his soul. When he is so completely possessed by animalistic traits that the soul takes on the appearance of a beast, he can be classified according to the nature of his soul and may in a sense be termed an animal.

Pythagoras, going even more deeply into the occult conditions resulting from a depraved life (which, it must be remembered, is an expression covering a multitude of acts), declared that as like attracts like and men incline towards natures most closely resembling their own, it was natural for the virtuous to incline towards God and for the vicious to incline towards the beast.

In fact, under certain circumstances, he suggested that a depraved human soul might attach itself to an animal, very much as a daemon might attach itself to a man. The human soul did not actually enter into the body of the animal but rather verged towards the instinctive nature of the animal in an effort to gratify its own uncurbed desires. (You may find yourself wondering what Hogarth would have made of this theme . . .) In other words, an animal could be moved or influenced by a human soul. But the "human" soul, the anti-transmigrationists insisted, could not conceivably enter into the body of the animal—a fine distinction, worthy of the rhetoricians of the day.

One further point before we continue.

It must be remembered that there was also a general acceptance of the concept of the incarnation of deeds and the building of bodies composed of actions.

Plato had already affirmed that man as a form proceeded from the sensations. It is important to bear in mind that all thought, feeling and action, having their origin in the supraphysical sphere, can be said to manifest as entities upon the planes of the inferior universe.

In a symbolic sense, insects were thus regarded as the incarnations of human attitudes, butterflies being an expression of the beautiful thoughts of men while those insects that tormented man and beast alike were said to be the offspring of destructive impulses of the soul. Plagues were attributed to a similar origin, the bacilli causing them being minute organisms brought into life by the emotions of men. Manifold orders of life, which were actually the mental and emotional progeny of human beings, were thus held to exist in the invisible world. Paracelsus had this in mind when he described the incubus and the succubus—the demons, male and female, fashioned from the stuff of emotional excess.

Many, particularly in the West, see re-embodiment (or Reincarnation) as meaning that the same being comes back to life again and again in new bodies, retaining its selfness at all times. This, however, is not so. The continuity of embodiment rests not with the embodiment of a spirit but with the perpetuation of *attitudes*. The individual who lives and dies with excessive pride will not be reborn in the personality of his former life, but it is his pride that is reborn. His pride takes on another body, which also develops excessive pride and passes through all the sorrows and miseries of this; proud to the last, the individual passes on again. The pride may then again be re-embodied, because it represents a negative force which must be worn out before the true being can incarnate.

Re-embodiment or rebirth is thus simply the coming into incarnation of the imperfections of a character. What must then be done is to reduce these imperfections and strengthen the constructive nature of the person. We are reminded that Plotinus took the attitude that his embodiment or rebirth was simply a monument to his own imperfection, and he did not wish it glorified.

It seems clear than that only through the gradual conquest of the negations in ourselves can we ultimately come to what can be described as a condition of peace and security. The more the positive and constructive circumstances dominate, the more the incarnation will be serene and, let us say, purposeful.

The morality of Reincarnation is simply that the individual is predestined to improve. He must grow spiritually, and any interference with this process of growth will result in suffering, the resistance of attitudes towards this need for growth. The mistakes for which we suffer are the attitudes that stand between us and integrity.

If you believe in Reincarnation, you believe in a purposeful life based upon the conquest of illusion within yourself. You take stock of yourself, estimate your needs, and realize that there is no way to avoid the duties which are proper to life. You study the factors of mental interference with integrity. You observe the pressure of emotional intensities that disturb integrity, and the degree to which you are self-hypnotizing your mind and diluting your life. You begin to estimate the true importance of your own thoughts and attitudes and, if you are wise, you come to the conclusion that your thoughts are important only if they are important thoughts—no amount of trivia can justify the function of the human mind. You begin then to determine, as best as you can, how you can use this mind, and settle down to planning a useful present life. The real reason for embodiment is after all not satisfaction, but the strengthening of the inner resources.

Reincarnation emphasizes this point that the individual always *does* have the opportunity to grow. His happiness or misery depend upon whether he accepts or rejects this opportunity.

In this book however we will not be concerned with the incarnations of human attitudes or deeds, but instead with what happens to that indefinable and intangible Self which man, for thousands of years, has called by so many names.

There are few faiths that have not recognized the existence of this Self, as for that matter even materialistic Science has come to do. The words will differ but, as we shall see, there has been and there still is a common awareness of its existence.

One thing you must remember in considering Reincarnation is that it is of course not you—the physical you, the visible you—that reincarnates. In other words, Reincarnation does not mean that you are going to return in a new body, retaining your personality, retaining your selfness, retaining the drives and compulsions that made you what you were.

No. It isn't that simple.

What returns is that which has animated you—that which has given you the ability to reason and to think and, if this is in your nature, to sense something of the forces that surround us.

Furthermore, if you should be caused to remember a past life, or even a moment out of that past life, what you are remembering or recollecting is not *your* past life, but a former life of the spirit within you when for a brief while, as history reckons it, this spirit, etheric or otherwise, dwelled in that host-body until it was time to leave it.

You are in other words, if I may so phrase it, not the master of your soul, but the *host* to your soul. It rests with you, as it will rest with others after you, whether this soul is to continue to be imprisoned within the human body, or whether it will finally attain the peace denied it in life after life.

This then is your responsibility—to live according to your faith, assuming you have one—and to not fear but to welcome the release represented by Death.

We here in the West fear Death, largely because we know nothing of the worlds outside our physical ken. We have incorporated half-forgotten memories of the race in our rituals and in our approach to the subject itself, translating our concept of the After Life into the language of our dogmas instead of into the language of the philosophic verities.

And so we fear Death, even when we talk of Brother Death, because for the past thousand years, and particularly in these last three hundred years, we have turned our back on our own Past and on its message.

We know the answers. Or we are confident that we do.

As a result, we face uncertain Tomorrows, armed in our philosophic ignorance, our wooden lances at the ready.

But what *do* we really mean when we talk of Reincarnation?

Let us ignore for the moment that in India, as in Egypt, Reincarnation was at the root of ethics. That the *Zohar* speaks of souls as being subject to transmigration: "All souls are subject to revolution (*a'leen b'gilgoolah*), but men do not know the ways of the Holy One; blessed be it! they are ignorant of the way they have been judged in all time, and before they came into this world and when they had quitted it." The Fathers of the Church, the Philosophic Gnostics and Neo-Platonists, the Mayas in the West, are among those who believed in Reincarnation, as did, in more recent times, the

Cambridge Platonists and Swedenborg and Schopenhauer and still others.

What *did* they believe in?

The entry of a psyche or "soul" into successive "bodies" of flesh.

Reincarnation and Metempsychosis (or Transmigration) are words which denote a concept of existence according to which a form of visible matter is inhabited by a more ethereal principle, which outlives its physical encasement and, on the death of the latter, passes on—either immediately or after an interval—to dwell in some other frame.

The concept of Reincarnation thus asserts the existence of a living and individualized Principle that dwells in and informs the body of a man and which, on the death of this body, passes into another body, after a longer or shorter interval. Successive bodily lives are thus linked together, to quote Annie Besant, "like pearls strung upon a thread, the thread being the living Principle, the pearls upon it the separate human lives."

What *is* this living something, this persistent reincarnating Principle?

You will be given a number of apparently contradictory explanations throughout this book, for there have obviously been divergences of opinion according to the orientation of the schools of thought described. When for instance a Theosophist speaks of Man, our real Human Self, this is of course not a reference to our physical and visible self, but to the reincarnating Ego. When therefore someone tells you, "My body is hungry", or "My body is tired", and not "I am hungry", or "I am tired", this is philosophically truer to fact than our self-identification with our body. We need to identify ourselves in thought not with the body in which we live, but with the Self that dwells therein.

The physical or animal nature of man is defined as consisting of four distinguishable parts or principles: the body, the etheric double, the vitality, and the passional nature—passions, appetites and desires. This physical or animal-man is influenced by the reincarnating Ego which imparts to this lower nature such of its own capacities as that animal-man is capable of assimilating. These capacities, working in and through the human brain, are recognized by us as the brain-mind or, if we are Theosophists, as the lower mind. Reason, judgment, memory, will, ideation (if we may term it that), as these faculties are known to us when the brain is in full activity, are the result of the influence of the reincarnating Ego, modified by the material conditions through which it must work. These conditions include healthy nerve-cells, properly balanced development of the respective groups of nerve cells, a full supply of blood containing nutritive matter that can be assimilated by the cells so as to supply waste, and carrying oxygen easily set free from its vehicles. If these conditions, or any of them, are absent, the brain cannot function. Thought processes can no more be carried out through such a brain than a melody can be produced from an organ the bellows of which are broken. The brain no more produces the thought than the organ produces the melody; in both cases, if we may phrase it that way, there is a player working through the instrument. But the power of the player to manifest himself, in thought or in melody, is limited by the capacities of the instrument at hand.

And here we come to what is as far as many are concerned the crux of the problem.

When we are born, the reincarnating Ego (some would call it the true Man) is linked to us, almost certainly while we are still in our mother's womb. This reincarnating Ego influences us through our brain, incarnation after incarnation, remaining one. It informs in turn men and women of different races and stations in life, and in each reaps experience, through each gathers knowledge, from each takes the material it supplies, weaving all this into its own eternal Being. It is this reincarnating Ego alone that can look back along the line of its rebirths, remember each earthly life, the story of each life from the cradle to the grave, century after century. You, as a physical "you," can neither look back on nor remember "your" rebirths, for you have actually never been born before, nor have your eyes seen the light of earlier days. But the innate character that is yours, the character with which you came into the world, is the character wrought and hammered out by a number of men and women who have lived before you, in successive lives, over a period of centuries or perhaps millennia.

In other words, *you*, the true *you*, the inner *you*, does remember these past lives, but the physical *you*, the, if you wish, animal-man, does not. This you, the visible you, the you that walks and talks and harumphs and pontificates and may even plead for understanding, lives only for the visible present, from day to day, from week to week, from year to year.

The only time that you will begin to even sense the possibility that "you" have had these former lives is if you are—either by adhering to a metaphysical discipline or by other means that we will touch on later in this book—aided in remembering or recollecting these past lives. In time you will understand that this was simply one of the garments the Self had worn before, no more identifiable with that self than the coat you wear on a raw and blustery night can be said to be a part of yourself. A man does not regard his coat as part of himself, because he is consciously able to take it off and look at it separated from himself. When you can do this with your body, calmly and consciously, assuming you have arrived at this conclusion after appropriate studies; not only does certainty become complete, but you will attain a certain inner peace, as have others in the past, as may others in the future.

You will find in this book that there have been a number of explanations of what can perhaps be called the method of Reincarnation. The disturbing thing about these explanations is that allowing for differences in language and approach—a Buddhist and a Neo-Platonist and a Christian Mystic will employ different word-images—there is a basic agreement between the teachers of the past and of the near-present.

The reincarnating Ego within the physical man has for example been called the Fifth Principle in man. This Fifth

Principle in the microcosm, man, answers to the Fifth Plane of the macrocosm, the universe outside man.

These planes are differentiations of primary substance and consciousness works on each plane through the conditions, whatever they may be, of each plane. Substance is here used to express Existence in its earliest objective form and has in it the potentiality of all, of most ethereal Spirit, of densest Matter.

Kosmos is evolved out of this primary Substance, which at its rarest is Spirit, Energy, Force, and at its densest the most solid Matter, every varying form in all worlds being of this Substance, aggregated into more or less dense masses, instinct with more or less Force.

When we talk of a plane we are only talking about a stage of existence in which this Spirit-Matter varies within certain limits, and acts under certain specific "laws". When we talk about the physical plane, we are thus talking about our visible, audible, tangible, odorous world, in which we come into contact with what we call Spirit-Matter, or Force and Matter, by way of the senses. Each plane is distinguishable by the characteristics of Spirit-Matter. On each of these planes, which interpenetrate each other, consciousness shows itself, working through the Spirit-Matter of that plane.

The reincarnating Ego within us has, as I said, been called the Fifth Principle in man, corresponding to the fifth plane of the universe outside man, the Kosmos, the Universal Mind, from which proceeds directly the molding, guiding, directing Force which is the essence of the forces on the physical plane. All the world of form, be it subtle or dense, is evolved by and through this Force of the Universal Mind, integrating the atoms into forms, disintegrating them again, building up and pulling down, constructing and destroying, attracting and repelling. From this fifth plane comes all the creation of forms, using the word creation in the sense of shaping pre-existent material, fashioning it into new forms, similar in a sense to the ability of the Adept to project into and materialize in the visible world the forms that his imagination has constructed out of inert cosmic matter in the invisible world.

The Adept is creating nothing new, but only utilizing and manipulating materials which Nature has in store around him, choosing what he wants and recalling it into an altered but objective existence.

Can the invisible become visible? Can we talk of a form gradually densifying as it passes from one world to the astral and from the astral to the physical? Annie Besant, writing in the 1890's, suggested you "think of a glass receiver, apparently empty, but in reality filled with the invisible gases, hydrogen and oxygen; a spark causes combination and 'water' exists there, but in a gaseous state; the receiver is cooled, and gradually a steamy vapour becomes visible; then the vapour condenses on the glass as drops of water; then the water congeals and becomes a film of solid ice crystals."

This process of condensation of rarer into grosser matter is actually something that happens all around us. The vegetable world grows by intaking gases from the atmosphere; everything around us, the plants we know, the herbs we use, the flowers we admire, exemplifies this orderly process within nature. So, too, do events develop on one plane (as passionate or emotional thoughts) and then take on astral form, and finally appear objectively as acts or events on the physical plane, the effects of pre-existing mental causes; the body can be held to be such an effect, molded on the etheric double. Try then to visualize in your own mind this body of etheric matter, serving as a mold into which denser matter may be built, using the word in a metaphysical sense. If the method of Reincarnation is to be understood at all, this conception of the dense body as the result of the "building" of dense molecules into a pre-existing etheric mold must, for the present, be accepted.

You must begin with assuming, very much as the Ancients did, that you are not talking about one body. When death comes to you, the subtler bodies will free themselves from the physical, the etheric double (according to one school of thought) disintegrating gradually with its dense frame. The thought-body (you will find later that there are other terms for this) which has resulted from the life just past lingers for a considerable time, going through various processes of assimilation of thoughts and experiences, handing on its conclusions to what may be termed the causal body, or reincarnating Ego, after which it, in turn, disintegrates.

As the period for Reincarnation approaches, the reincarnating Ego builds a new mental and a new astral body, while it is provided with a mold suited to the Karma or destiny to be worked out, and after this the etheric double is "built." Since the brain, in common with the rest of the dense body, is "built" into this etheric double, this brain is, to all practical purposes, the physical expression, however imperfect, of the mental qualities and habits of the human being about to be incarnated, the fitting physical vehicle for the exercise of the capacities which his experience in past lives now enables him to manifest on this physical plane.

The determining factor is the experience, or more precisely the experiences, of the past lives. If you continually give birth to thought-forms of selfishness, desires for self, hopes for self, plans for self, and these forms clustering around you react against you (not in the usual sense, but in the karmic sense), your character hardens into a type which in due course is given etheric form as the mold for "your" next dense body. Your new dense body will be built into this etheric mold which reflects this character of yours, and the brain takes on the shape physically needed for the continued gratification of these tendencies. Throughout this new life the past will dominate the present and possibly for many more lives will you have to come back and come back again in an effort to undo the damage done to your reincarnating Ego by your past actions in a to-you unknown past.

On the other hand, assuming you continually, in this life, give birth to thought-forms of unselfishness, helpful desires for others, loving plans for the welfare of others, earnest hopes for the good of others, these thought forms will cluster around you and react on you, and when you die your character will have become ingrainedly unselfish. Here we have the cause of the "building" of the benevolent and philanthropic type of brain for the succeeding incarnation. Thus, step by step, is brought about the evolution of man, character being molded in personality after personality, the gains and losses governing the succeeding physical manifestations.

In other words, if you agree this is so, you agree with the Ancients that you can influence the ultimate destiny of this reincarnated Ego.

When we talk of the etheric body, as we will, using these or other words, throughout this book, we are talking about a Hermetic concept which antedates the Neo-Platonists and was one of the long-ignored axioms and formulae rediscovered during the Middle Ages and, still later, by Theophrastus of Hohenheim, who called himself Paracelsus.

His belief that nearly all diseases have their origin in what was conceived of as the invisible nature of man was a fundamental precept of Hermetic medicine. While Hermetists in no way disregarded the physical body, they believed that man's material constitution was an emanation from, or, if we may term it that way, an objectification of, his invisible spiritual principles.

There is one vital substance in nature upon which all things subsist. It has been called *archaeus* or vital life force, and is synonymous with the astral light or spiritual air of the ancients.

This vital energy has its origin in the spiritual body of the earth.

Every created thing has two bodies, according to the Hermetists—one visible and substantial, the other invisible and transcendent. The latter consists of an ethereal counterpart of the physical form. The vehicle of *archaeus* can be described as a vital body. This etheric "shadow sheath" is not dissipated by death but remains until the physical form is totally disintegrated. It is derangements of this astral light body that can cause much disease. Paracelsus, who died in 1541, taught that a person with a morbid mental attitude could poison his own etheric nature and that this infection, affecting the natural flow of vital life force, would later take the form of a physical ailment. Plants and minerals likewise had an invisible nature composed of this vital life force, but each would manifest it in a different way.

James Gaffarel, writing in 1650 on the astral-light bodies of flowers, said that though they might be chopped into pieces, pounded in a mortar or even burnt to ashes, they still retained, both in the juice and in the ashes, the self-same figure that they'd had before, and that though it might at first not be visible, they could be made visible to the eye under certain conditions.

He quotes the story told by a contemporary, the Sieur de la Violette, "one of the best chymists that our age hath produced," who knew a Polish physician in Krakow who kept the ashes of almost all the herbs that were known in glasses in his laboratory.

If you should, out of curiosity, wish to see one of them—say the rose—he would hold the glass containing the ashes of the rose over a lighted candle. As soon as it began to feel the heat, you could see the ashes begin to move, "which afterwards rising up and dispersing themselves about the glass, you should immediately observe a kind of little dark cloud which, dividing itself into many parts, it came at length to represent a rose, but so fair, so fresh, so perfect a one, that you would have thought it to have been as substantial and as odiferous a rose as grows on the rose tree."

Paracelsus, considering derangements of the etheric double as the most important cause of disease, attempted to reharmonize the substances of this etheric double by bringing it into contact with other bodies whose vital energy could supply the needed elements or would be strong enough to overcome the diseased conditions existing in the aura of the sufferer. Upon the removal of the invisible cause of the disease, the ailment would speedily vanish.

Paracelsus called the vehicle for the vital life force the *mumia.* The most universal form of this mumia was ether, and the medical system of Paracelsus was based on the concept that by removing this diseased etheric mumia from the organism of the patient (possibly in the manner described elsewhere in this book by Dr. Denys Kelsey, but more likely by causing it or by seeming to cause it to be accepted into the nature of a plant or animal), it would be possible to divert from the patient the flow of the vital life force which had been nourishing the illness.

According to the Hermetic philosophers there were seven primary causes of disease. The first was evil spirits, creatures born of degenerate actions, subsisting on the vital energies of those to whom they attached themselves. The second cause was a derangement of the spiritual nature and the material nature—the failure of these two to coordinate would produce mental and physical subnormality. The third cause was an unhealthy and abnormal mental attitude. Melancholia, morbid emotions, passions, lusts, greeds and hates, would affect the vehicle for the vital life force, from which they reacted into the physical body, resulting in ulcers, tumors, cancers, fevers and tuberculosis. The fourth cause of disease was what we know as Karma, the Law of Compensation, which demanded that the individual pay in full for the misdeeds of past lives. A physician had to be careful how he interfered with the workings of this law, in view of the possibility that he might be thwarting the plan of Eternal Justice. The fifth cause was the motions and aspects of the heavenly bodies. Hermetists taught that a strong and wise man ruled his stars, but that a negative and weak person would be ruled by them. The sixth cause of disease could be a misuse of faculty, organ, or function, such as overstraining a member or overtaxing the nerves. The seventh cause was the presence in the system of foreign substances, impurities or obstructions, caused either by diet, air, sunlight, or the presence of foreign bodies.

Disease could be prevented, according to the Hermetists, by spells and invocations, by vibration (the inharmonies of the bodies could be neutralized by chanting spells and intoning the sacred names, or by playing upon musical instruments and singing). Other methods involved the use of talismans, charms and amulets; the administration of herbs and simples (having determined by the stars the sickness and the cause, the doctors then prescribed the herbal antidote); and by prayer. Paracelsus said that faith could cure all disease. In the next breath, almost anticipating times to follow, he added that few persons possessed a sufficient degree of faith.

For many years, Christian mystics have recognized, as did the Hermetists, the existence of this etheric body or double to which Paracelsus referred. While this concept, it must be understood, is common to both East and West, it so happens that in these days Western interpreters, or paraphrasers, have made the words, perhaps more than the inner meaning, familiar to students of metaphysics, particularly in this country.

When we thus talk of the spiritual nature of man, we are told that the physical nature itself is the result of spiritual activity. All that is objectively seen is but the outward manifestation of inner subjective energies. While the scientist is concerned with the mechanics of the cosmos and of man, the metaphysically oriented Christian, generally the student of a somewhat watered-down school of thought whose claims to metaphysical authority are at times debatable, has a number of attitudes concerning this concept of the etheric body.

There is nothing but energy, and it functions through a substance which interpenetrates and actuates all forms and which is analogous to the ether of the modern world. Matter is energy and spirit in its densest form, and spirit is matter in its most sublimated aspect.

As all forms are interpenetrated by this ether, every form has an etheric form or etheric body.

There are positive centers of force in every etheric body in the midst of negative substance. The human being has an etheric body which is positive to the negative physical body, which galvanizes it into activity, and acts as its coherent force, holding it in being.

The etheric body of man has seven principal nuclei of energy through which various types of energy flow, producing his psychical activity. These nuclei are related to the cerebro-spinal system, and the base of this psychical activity, or the seat of the nature of the soul, is situated in the head. The entire mechanism can be directed from this center, and energized through the medium of the other six force centers.

Only certain centers are now functioning in man. The rest are quiescent. In a perfect human being all centers function fully to produce perfect psychical unfoldment.

But what is this etheric body?

Is it something that you can touch or see and instantly recognize for the alien thing it must be, assuming we have the conventional Western approach to this question?

What is it, you say? A universal substance, the source of everything, but so sublimated, so subtle, that it is beyond the grasp and the comprehension of most of us. As Alice A. Bailey put it, "in comparison with it, the most delicate fragrance, the dancing radiance of sunbeams, the crimson glory of the sunset, are gross and earthly. It is 'a web of light,' forever invisible to human eye." *

Subtle and fugitive as this universal substance may be, it is at the same time even denser than matter. Complementing the factors which we recognize as a part of us, the interaction of these life forces results in that intangible something which we call "consciousness" or "soul" and which all religions and schools of thought have known of and held to be peculiarly their own.

We can say, with considerable justice, that the entire manifested world arises from energy and from its co-factors, substance and consciousness. All that is seen, from the sands in the desert to the stars in the heavens, from man at the most primitive level to a Buddha or a Christ, is an outgrowth of this energy. Matter is energy in its densest or lowest form; spirit is this same energy in its highest or most subtle form.

In taking on density, energy takes on or descends into seven planes. Man personifies three of these—he has his physical body, his emotional mechanism, and his mind-body. He can function on all three planes, and is on the threshold

* pps. 51-52, in *The Soul and Its Mechanism* (1930, Lucis, New York).

of recognition of a fourth and higher plane, that of the soul or self.

The physical body of man has its etheric counterpart, its etheric body. Positive in nature, while the dense physical body is negative, the etheric body is the cohesive factor, maintaining the physical body in its existence.

The etheric counterpart, whether of man or of any other physical thing, partakes of the universal substance, life and energy. But it is neither self-sufficient nor independently existing. It draws upon the reservoir of universal energy and in it the etheric counterpart lives and moves and has its being. Energy is thus functioning through the etheric, just as much as the universal energy functions through man's etheric body. And as man exists or can exist on seven planes, assuming he be fully developed, similarly his etheric body has seven points of contact with energy, though normally only three force-centers are fully developed.

As Sir Oliver Lodge and many others have pointed out, we can thus proceed from the assumption that every sensible object (i.e., which can be seen or bumped into or touched or felt) has both a material and an etheric counterpart. There are a variety of names for it but, with the subject of this book in mind, there is some point to quoting Dr. C.E.M. Joad's comment on what he calls "the life force," and describes as being far from all-powerful. "It is limited," Joad says, "by the matter which it seeks to overcome, and its methods are experimental, varying according to the stage of evolution which, in the persons of the organisms created by it, it has succeeded in reaching. Different types of beings best serve its purpose at different stages." *

Thus we find that behind the objective body which we know and are aware of there lies a subjective form constituted of etheric matter and acting as a conductor of the life principle of energy. This life principle can be described as the force aspect of the soul. Through the medium of the etheric body, the soul animates the form, gives it its peculiar qualities

* pp. 179, C.E.M. Joad, *Mind and Matter,* as quoted by Alice A. Bailey.

and attributes, impresses its desires upon it, and directs it through the activity of the mind. Through the medium of the brain, the soul galvanizes the body into conscious activity, while through the medium of the heart, all parts of the body are pervaded to and, in a sense, given life.

We have seen how the three states of man's nature—physical, sentient, and mental—form a coordinated one. The directing self, acting through the mind on the vital or etheric body, can now guide us towards frontiers which, if not wholly new, are at least new to these days.

But what *do* we mean when we talk about the soul?

It has been treated as an entity, manifested in man's volitional thinking activities; it is not the mind but the soul that thinks and wills.

At the same time, in a carry-over from late 18th century thought, the soul has been considered to be a function or the sum of the functions of the brain, and thus identified with but not the inspirer of the mind.

Plato believed the soul to have three parts—an immortal or rational part, coming or stemming from God; a mortal, animal or sensitive part, the seat of appetite and sensation, belonging to the body; and a third part, lying between these two and making their interaction possible. He regarded this rational soul as immaterial and metaphysical in nature, incapable of being perceived by the senses, and only to be grasped by the intellect.

There is the Aristotelian concept of the soul as the sum of the vital principles and as being to the body what vision is to the eye, the true Being in the body or, as Plotinus saw it, the living sentiency of the body, belonging to a higher degree of being than matter.

While he held that the soul could not be said to have parts, St. Gregory, in the 4th century, did distinguish nutritive, sensitive, and rational faculties, corresponding to the body, soul and spirit. The soul united with the body was seen as the real source of all activities.

The animist approach, in the 17th century, regarded the

body as made for the soul and emphatically not the product of the soul, with the soul the source of all vital movement. The immediate cause of death was not disease but the action of the soul in leaving the bodily machine; either it had become unworkable through some serious lesion, or because it did not choose to animate it any longer.

The soul and the self are synonymous terms in Oriental literature. As Radakrishnan has pointed out, ". . . 'soul' belongs to every being that has life in it, and the different souls are fundamentally identical in nature. The differences are due to the physical organizations that obscure and thwart the life of the soul. The nature of the bodies in which the souls are incorporated accounts for their various degrees of obscuration." In a subsequent passage echoing the conclusions of the many teachers whose opinions we will share with you in this book, he further points out that, "Every ego possesses within the gross material body, which suffers dissolution at death, a subtle body, formed of the psychical apparatus, including the senses." *

We are concerned at this point not with the semantics of metaphysics, which fallible minds have, from time to time, produced or taught, but with the obvious possibility that matter is spirit or energy in its lowest manifestation, and spirit is matter in its highest expression. From the emergence of the human family, as it is so optimistically termed, there has been a paralleling development of the God concept to account for nature, and the soul concept to account for man, with speculation rife, to put it mildly, as to where the soul might be found.

Plato held that the vital principle was in the brain and that the brain and the spinal cord were the coordinators of the vital force. Hippocrates, Galen and St. Augustine likewise saw the soul as being located in the brain (in the case of St. Augustine, in the middle ventricle). Roger Bacon considered the center of the brain to be the place where the soul could be found, while Swedenborg saw the "the royal road of the

* quoted by Alice A. Bailey. p. 74.

sensations of the body to the soul" as being through the *corpora striata,* a pair of large ganglia of the brain, immediately under the frontal and upper region of the brain.

In more recent times there has been less emphasis on this question of the probable location of the soul, and more concern with the relation of psychical qualities to the brain. Parallel with this, and with the rise in the West of schools of thought which can be loosely described as both metaphysical and essentially Christian in nature, there is greater response to the older concept of the triplicity of soul, mind and brain.

We also find ourselves coming closer to accepting the concept that the universe is composed of two materials, one of them the sonoriferous ether or *Akasa* of the Kenopanishad. Swami Vivekananda described it as the "omnipresent all penetrating existence. Everything that has form, everything that is the result of the compounds, is evolved out of this *Akasa.* It is the *Akasa* that becomes the air, that becomes the liquids, that becomes the solids; it is the *Akasa* that becomes the sun, the earth, the moon, the stars, the comets; it is the *Akasa* that becomes the body, the animal body, the planets, every form that we see, everything that can be sensed, everything that exists. It itself cannot be perceived; it is so subtle that it is beyond all ordinary perception; it can only be seen when it has become gross, taken form. At the beginning of creation there is only this *Akasa;* at the end of the cycle the solids, the liquids, and the gases all melt again into the *Akasa,* and the next creation similarly proceeds out of this *Akasa.*" *

* as quoted by Alice A. Bailey, pps. 85-86.

II

THE BUDDHIST AND INDO-PLATONIC APPROACH

In the first sermon of the Lord Buddha to the five ascetics in the deer park of Sarnath he said:

"Open your ears, O monks. Deliverance from mortality is found. I teach, I preach the Dharma. If you walk according to my teachings you will be partakers in a short time of that for which sons of nobles will leave their homes and go to the homeless life—the highest end of religious effort; you will even in this present time apprehend the truth itself and see it face to face.

"There are two extremes, O monks, which the truth-seeker ought to avoid; the first one is a life of sensualism which is low, ignoble, vulgar, unworthy and unprofitable; the other is a life of extreme asceticism, which is painful, unworthy and unprofitable.

"However, there is a Middle Path, discovered by the Tathāgata *, a path which opens the eyes and bestows understanding, which leads to peace of mind, to higher wisdom, to full enlightenment, to eternal peace, 'Nirvāna.' This Middle Path which the Tathāgata has discovered is the noble Eightfold Path (Astānga marga), Right Understanding, Right Thought, Right Speech, Right Action, Right Livelihood, Right Effort, Right Mindfulness and Right Meditation.

"This is the Middle Path which the Tathāgata

* Buddha.

has discovered, which is the path which opens the eyes, bestows understanding, which leads to peace of mind, to higher wisdom, to perfect enlightenment, to eternal peace—'Nirvāna.'

"Birth is attended with pain, old age is painful, disease is painful, death is painful, association with the unpleasant is painful, separation from the pleasant is painful, the non-satisfaction of one's desire is painful, in brief, the coming into existence is painful. This is the Noble Truth of suffering.

"Verily it is that clinging to life which causes the renewal of rebirth, accompanied by several delights, seeking satisfaction now here, now there—that is to say, the craving for a gratification of the passions, or the craving for a continuity of individual existence or the craving for annihilation. This is the Noble Truth of the origin of suffering.

"And the Noble Truth of the cessation of suffering consists in the destruction of passions, the destruction of all desires, the laying aside of, the getting rid of, the being free from, the harboring no longer of this thirst. And the Truth which points the way is the Noble Eightfold Path. This is the foundation of a world of Righteousness, Peace and Happiness."

You can almost hear the calm and even voice as, turning to ignorance of the four Noble Truths, he explained to the ascetics the chain of Inter-dependent Origination (pratitya samutpāda, in Sanskrit):

"On ignorance depend moral and immoral thoughts and deeds and bodily and vocal expressions; on moral and immoral thoughts and deeds and bodily and vocal expressions depends consciousness; on consciousness depends material and immaterial factors of an individual; on material and immaterial factors of an individual depends the six organs of senses; on the six organs of senses de-

pends contact; on contact depends sensation; on
sensation depends desire; on desire depends attachment; on attachment depends becoming; on becoming depends birth; on birth depends old age, death,
sorrow, lamentation, misery, grief and despair."

When Buddhists say that the Lord Buddha was endowed
with the Divine Eye and Divine Ear, this means that he was
gifted with clairvoyance and clairaudience. He also possessed
these further qualities: he was devoid of greed, hate and ignorance; he was the All-Enlightened One, endowed with supreme wisdom and the best conduct; he was the knower of
the universe and was supreme in taming men; and, in addition to being the teacher of gods and men, he was, Buddhists
say, Omniscient and Holy.

Buddha preached the Arya Dharma for forty-five years in
India. Essentially a reformer, he was preaching a Middle
Path rather than a new and extreme doctrine. This Middle
Path, or the Noble Eightfold Path, was Right Understanding,
Right Thought, Right Speech, Right Action, Right Liveli-
hood, Right Effort, Right Mindfulness and Right Meditation.

By Right Understanding is meant the realization of the
four Noble Truths as explained in his first sermon:

"This is suffering; this is the cause of suffering;
this is the cessation of suffering and this is the path
that leads to the cessation of suffering."

Right Thought meant the aspiration or resolve to free one-
self from selfish desires, from anger and hate and to fill one-
self with compassion for all living beings.

Right Speech is the absence of falsehood and of words that
cause hate and anger and are harsh or profane. Meaningless
speech, blackmailing, slander and deceitfulness and boastful
talk are excluded as not being in accord with Right Speech.

Right Action is the abstaining from killing, injuring, or in-
citing the killing of any living being; and the abstaining from
theft and adultery, from drunkenness and gambling.

Right Livelihood is the abstaining from all modes of life which involve wrong speech and action, and also the abstaining from trading in weapons and opium and other harmful drugs and poisons, as well as in living beings, and in meat and fish. In other words, a true Buddhist can never be a butcher, hunter or a fisherman; nor can he be connected in any way with the practise of vivisection or with the use of animals, as both we and the Russians have done, in space research.

Right Effort is fourfold; the effort, when no immoral thought has arisen, to prevent it from arising; when an immoral thought has arisen, to get rid of that immoral thought; when a moral thought has not arisen, to endeavor that the moral thought may arise; and when the moral thought has arisen, to develop the moral thought.

Right Mindfulness is mindfulness or watchfulness about the body or any part of the body, also mindfulness about feeling, mindfulness about speech, and mindfulness about thought.

Right Meditation has four stages. The first stage is the feeling of joy and pleasure free from passion and evil thoughts. The second stage is the feeling of joy and pleasure free from reasoning and investigation. The third stage is the feeling of equanimity towards joy and pleasure. The fourth stage is the feeling with no pleasure and no pain but with the purity of mindfulness and equanimity.

As long as he did not have "the absolute true knowledge" of these four Noble Truths, the Buddha continued in his sermon to the ascetics, he had not acknowledged that he had gained "the Incomparable Supreme Enlightenment". It was not until it became perfectly clear to him that he had attained this knowledge that there came to him the knowledge:

"Unshakable is the deliverance of my mind, this
is my last birth, now there is no more rebirth."

As far as Buddhists are concerned, the Truth set forth in this first sermon can be considered as the basis of all of the Buddha's later teachings. In the four Noble Truths and in the

Noble Eightfold Path, they find the true way for an escape
from the misery of Samsāra, the ceaseless round of birth and
death.

This is reflected in the famous hymn of Chojo Tsang-pa
known as the *Religious Wishes*, which, you were enjoined,
must be said in a spirit of disinterestedness, believing that the
prayer-hymn is being listened to and approved.

"By my own merit and that of all other sentient
beings acquired in all the three times, may I be
born for the sake of all (comprising those in
Nirvāna and Samsāra) in all my future lives, as a
free and well-endowed human being, which is a
precious boon.

"In all my future lives, may I be one of the foremost among those of great faith. May I be the foremost amongst the meek. Foremost among the zeal-
ous and intelligent. Foremost amongst those of
great aspirations, and of great learning.

"May I be foremost amongst the compassionate
ones. Foremost amongst the understanding ones,
and amongst the persevering ones; foremost among
the hard-working ones.

"May I ever be possessed of a mind well versed
in all branches of knowledge, which is the property
of a divine mind. May I ever meet with profound
scholars and professors of the Mahayanic doctrine,
as soon as I am born.

"Let their threefold benedictions and blessings
and virtues of the body, speech and heart enter
into my body, heart and speech completely, and inspire me. Let me ever be initiated among the
monks at the feet of Gurus, like the Buddha himself in my youth, in all my future lifetimes.

"May I ever be able to keep the vows and ob-
servances purely and strictly. May I be able to
learn, practise and observe all the branches of the
Dharma as they should be one, in pure spirit.

"Let me be thoroughly conversant with listening,

pondering, and meditating on the Mahayanic doctrine in all its branches. In learning, studying and practising the Dharma, let there be no impediments whatever, neither external nor internal.

"Let me be perfect in the attainment of knowledge. Let me be thoroughly conversant and competent in fulfilling the duties of my life. Let me, his son, be able to fill my Guru's place.

"Let me be habituated in feeling pity and in contemplating on Sūnyatā. Let me be able to accomplish my own and others' purposes. Let me obtain Divine inspiration.

"Let the gloom of Ignorance be cleared up. Let everything, whether good or bad, help me on the path to Buddhahood. By the merit of these wishes may I, by the power of great intellect, realize the Eternal Truth.

"By my great pity, let me not be apathetic to others' pangs and miseries. By great learning let me be able to implant learning or knowledge in others' hearts. By great experience let me be able to lead others on the path.

"By knowledge let myself be emancipated, by grace let me be able to save others. Let me be wise in combining circumstances: Let me be free as the sky from fixed assertions and dogmatic beliefs.

"Let the Karmic influences be portrayed in favourable circumstances. Let all selfish motives be eradicated. Let me be able to respect all sentient beings of the six realms alike, without any partiality.

"Let me be able to identify and recognize in the body, speech and mind of all the sentient beings of the three states of existence the presence of the three Divine principles of the Buddhas of the three times.

"Let me be able to regard my Guru with the same regard as I would regard a Buddha. And by the merit of this virtue let there be no contraction in my faith. Let my belief experience no break, and let me enjoy communion of spirit with my Guru.

"Let the graces, knowledge and virtue of the Buddha and Gurus enter and inspire me. Let all my faults be purged and let all the virtues be perfected in me. Let my heart be filled with the thought of 'no want'.

"Let my attachment be cut off from the roots. Let not my heart yearn or wish others' enjoyments. Let me obtain power over counteracting passions or impious impulses.

"Let me be able to clip and prune the heads of thoughts of worldly ambitions. Let me be able to bear happiness and sorrows equally. Let trials and tribulations prove my friends.

"Let all my objective thoughts turn out to be some spiritual duty. Let me get safely over the precipice of hope and fear. Let an impartial love to all grow up in me.

"Let me know all others as equal with myself. Let me be able to exchange happiness with misery. Let me be able to carry the griefs and pains of others with gladness and joy. Having shouldered them, let me be filled with compassion enough to bear them without grudging.

"Let me be put on the Path by the doorway of compassion. Let me be able to merge everything equally in the contemplation of Sūnyatā. Let the one prime and sole need be fulfilled in the right time.

"Let me have steadiness in tranquilizing my mind in Samadhi. Let me obtain the power of foreknowledge and other boundless siddhic powers of illusion. Let me be able to analyze Intellect to its very root. Let all cognitions appear to me as the Dharmakāya.

"Let all my credulous errors turn to divine inner lights. Let me be able to recognize Nirvāna in Samsāra. Let me obtain the highest boon of the great symbol Maha-mudra.* Let me be able to control all mental cognitions.

"Let me be able to keep Karmic connections without any impartiality. Let all those connections prove effective or fruitful of bringing forth useful results.

"Let all those actions which I might do, or have done to others in the three times, as well as those which others might do or have done to me in the three times, be they either useful or injurious, let them never bear evil results nor indifferent ones; let all the internal, external and side Karmic influences be cleared off this very moment.

"Henceforth let no carnality, wrath, sloth, pride or egoism, jealousy or envy, praise-seeking, and desire for fame, nor self-flattery, nor any kind of impious wish or thought, ever come in my mind.

"Let me be a fit vessel to receive the Mystic Truths.** Let me obtain the four kinds of empowering initiations. Let me be able to know the Divine Intuitions. Let me acquire familiarity in the meditation of the imaginary and the formless unimaginable—Rūpa and Arūpa, Forms and the Formless.

"Let me know the general and the minute laws of Karma. Let me know the logical process of Intellect. By the power of this merit may I, in this and in all the lifetimes, be able to perform my duties towards all sentient beings illimitably, and without my seeking it.

"Let me be able to perform these duties successfully by the path of the six virtues. Let me be able to accomplish unbounded good for all sentient

---

* In the earlier forms of Indian Buddhist Tantrism, Mahā-mudrā was represented as the eternal female principle symbolically by Advayavajra as free from the veils which cover the cognizable object, as shining forth like the serene sky at noon during autumn, and as "the identity of samsāra and nirvāna; her body is compassion which is not restricted to a single object; she is the uniqueness of Great Bliss."

** the mystic truths of the Tantras.

beings without feeling wearied or having any regret.

"Even after my death, let my head and limbs, flesh and bones, organs and minor organs, hair, teeth, nails, blood and secretions, oil and fat exuding from my body, all be of unbounded use and of great service to all sentient beings.

"May those who are, have been, or will be fond of me, loved me, respected me, and believed in me, and who may have prayed or entreated me in any way, or those who have followed me, obtain transcendental knowledge, in their hearts, without the least trouble.

"Let their experience of the divine inspiration continue in an unbroken current and remain permanently. Let him or them obtain transcendental Samādhi. Let him obtain the Divine and the temporal blessings without seeking for them.

"Let those who have disbelieved in the three times, scoffed and reviled at me, dispraised me, and have been envious of me, or who have born me ill will, or tried to quarrel with me, slandered me and abused me, let these go to chasten me of my evil actions and wash away the bad Karmic influences of the three times at once this very moment.

"Let those who may have wronged me not to have to suffer the Karmic effects of their actions, and let not such actions stand in the way of their obtaining Buddhahood. Let those very persons be converted by me, and let them obtain Buddhahood in this very lifetime or during one life.

"Let all those of my friends who have in all my states of existence helped to put me in the righteous path, obtain all the virtues of a Buddha and obtain Buddhahood.

"Let the life-term of my Gurus expand as wide as the heavens and last till the cessation of the Samsāra, until which event takes place, let not them rest in Nirvāna, in quiescense, but remain active for the sake of sentient beings.

"Let my body, speech and heart be filled with the

holy grace of the Buddhas, and those virtues by which they transcend common beings even in this very moment, and let my three-fold principles be perfected.

"For the sake of serving others, let me be accomplished in compounding eye-medicaments and pills, and obtain the eight Siddhic powers.* Let diseases, evil spirits, ignorance and other ill-wills of all sorts subside.

"Let me able to utilize all inborn thoughts, ignorance, devas and demons, samsāric troubles and miseries, sickness and death, in the path of emancipation. Let me be able to give up the idea of self-ish-existence as an individuality.

"Knowing that I am dying, and fully conscious of every circumstance attending it, let me die in a joyful and contended frame of mind. Recognizing the clear light even in the first stage of the uncertain state ** after death, let me attain Nirvāna for myself by absorbtion in the Dharma-kāya.

"Should I however have visions of the uncertain state of the intermediary state of existence after death, let me know that state to be the intervening state after death and before rebirth. Let me be able to look without fear on the Person of the Divine Clear Light.

"Let me acquire the power of recognizing those states or realms as my guardian deities. Let the flame of the clear light burn up all ideas and recollections of materialism. Let me have thorough control over reasoning intellect.

"Let me after deliberation choose such a birth which will be useful in the highest degree. Let me be gifted with the six powers of prescience.

"Let me have the prescient powers of a Deva's eyes. Let me have the prescient powers of a Deva's ears. Let me have the power of recollecting former

---

* supernatural powers.
 * *Bar-do,* the state between death and rebirth.

places in the future. Let me have the power of knowing others' thoughts. Let me have the power of knowing when I have attained the power of rendering my supernatural and illusive powers indestructible.

"Let me be gifted with the five visions or powers of seeing. Let all phenomena be utilized by me in the path. Let me be thoroughly practised in generating physical heat, and let bliss grow in me. Let warmth grow in me. Let my nerves and arteries be easy, and let the respirations be gentle. Let the uncognizing state grow in me.

"Let me acquire the clear light. Let me be thoroughly practised in the art of projection.* By means of the Samādhi on Truth let me be able to control phenomenal appearances.

"Let me be able to confound the perverted ones. Let me remember death and the hereafter. Let me be able to renounce this life. Let my mind be always ready for work.

"Let my heart always tend towards the Dharma. Let all my acts ever tend towards the Dharma. Let me never have a single irreligious thought. Let me be able to visit all hermitages and ascetic retreats without partiality.

"Let the limit of my term of existence be until the entire Samsāra is completely emptied; until then let me ever be working for the benefit of all sentient beings. Let all the fruits or results of my prayers fructify in this very lifetime.

"Let them again expand as wide as the heavens, and equal the Realms of Truth and the realms or circle of the Omniscient-who-knows all the three times.

"Let the result of my prayer last until the Samsāra gets emptied, and let them ever grow in great deeds in the fulfillment of the higher and lower paths.

* of the mind.

"In brief, by the power of these merits, let me be equal in every respect to every one of my lineal Gurus, Devas, Dākinīs, Dharmapāls, guardian deities, devotees, truly illumined ones, Yogis and others, including even the Buddhas and Bodhisattvas that existed, do exist, and will exist, in the three times and the ten directions.

"Let me equal them from this very moment in body, speech, mind, accomplishments or virtues, and in deeds, in duration of lifeterm and the expanse of realms, in the quality of divine deeds, in procreation of beings similar to myself, in wisdom and knowledge, in aspiration and courage, in divine knowledge, in grace and miracles, in prescience and in the extent of the work done."

To a great extent this revealing hymn, apart from illustrating the attitude towards Reincarnation of Buddhism, reflects the trend, in both Hinduism and Mahayana Buddhism of the Tibetan form, to consider it more essential to venerate the Guru who transmits to you the doctrine of the Holy Dharma than to worship a being who has long ago passed into the state of Nirvāna and is thus out of reach for veneration or prayers. He who is a transmitter of the Holy Dharma is to be venerated because he leads you and instructs you to follow the Path and to lead a life of purity. Through the mouth of this Guru, Lord Buddha speaks to you.

To the same extent, Tibetan Buddhism tells us that Jesus Christ, the ascetic who had been a pupil of both Hindu and Buddhist Gurus, described himself correctly as a Supreme Guru (or Teacher) through whose mouth God was speaking on the Law, very much as Moses, long before, had been the interpreter of the Law of God.

The *Pratītya Samutpāda*, or the twelve chains of Interdependent Origination, are represented in Tibetan symbolism as the Wheel of Life, also known as the Wheel of Becoming. In almost every monastery there would be a large painted Wheel of Life, illustrating the nature of *Samsāra*, the world of transmigration, with its six worlds or realms in which human beings can be reborn, the beginning made at the top and going around to the right. Behind the Wheel, the angry face of *Mahākāla* (The Great Time) can be seen biting with its teeth into the Wheel, symbolizing the 'Teeth of Time'. His two hands and feet are likewise grasping the Wheel. His head is covered by a crown of human skulls symbolizing the impermanence of human life.

Mahākāla, as a symbolic representation of Eternity, can be said to swallow the offender; in other words, the offender will, because of his sins, wander almost eternally in *Samsāra* and thus be chained on the Wheel of Life, or Time, for an almost limitless time. This round of births and deaths need not however be eternal for the individual since there is, the Buddhists say, the way of escape as shown by the Lord Buddha.

The six realms of transmigration are: the world of gods *, the world of demons, the realm of the hungry ghosts, the nether worlds (or lower states of life), the animal world and the world of human beings.

In the middle of the Wheel there is a representation of the root evils, of craving, hate and delusion, the origin of all Sāmsāric life, symbolized here by three animals. A red cock stands for greed or craving, a green snake for hate, and a black pig for delusion. These three animals are biting each other, forming an inner wheel or circle.

The pleasures enjoyed by the gods in the heavenly worlds are represented by music and dance. The trouble is that they at times tend to forget that they cannot forever continue to exist in this world of no sorrows; they will have to return to human life after what might be termed their stock of merits, resulting from good actions which caused their rebirth among the gods, is exhausted.

In the *Srī-cakrasambhāra* Tantra there is a passage suggesting that rebirth among the gods is not as desirable as it looks

---

* Hinduism says that Buddha was an *avatār* or the incarnation of the god Visnu, the ninth in the line. Buddha himself said that he had many times been a god in previous lives.

from the human point of view, for even the gods are subject to disease and death. Even worse, at the end of their time, the godly body fades, loses his brightness, gets a bad color, and an evil stench issues from the body, so much so that the other divine beings keep away from him.

The mental sufferings of a god who feels that he is on the way out of heaven are obviously great, for he doesn't know what to do in order to avoid being born again in the world of men with all its attendant sufferings. But there is no way out, and no karmic merit has accumulated during his sojourn among the gods, hence the Law of Karma, which does not exempt the gods, forces him back to this or another world where there are mortals. In other words, a rebirth among the gods, although possible, is not to be striven for, because such a rebirth will in actuality only delay the attainment of Buddhahood and *Nirvāna*.

In order to symbolize the opposite of heavenly pleasures the Tibetan artist will have painted a representation of what might be termed infernal tortures below the Wheel. These are however not punishments handed down by any Divine Judge. It is our own Karma, our own actions, say the Buddhists, that bring us to these infernal states of life. The Wheel of Life also represents birth, growth, mating, disease, old age and death; in other words, everything which you may have reason to anticipate in this or in future lives.

To conclude—you will recall that we are told in the *Mahābhārata*, the Indian Epic,

"He should be called a Brahmana who possesses these virtues, namely, truth, liberality, forgiveness, good conduct, mercy, pity and self-control."

In the Dhammapada we find verses which clearly demonstrate Buddha's opinion of caste, but also of what he called a *Brāhmana*, or Brahmin.

"A man is not a Brahmana by reason of his mat-

ted hair or his lineage or his caste; in whom are to
be found Truth and Law, he is Pure and him I call
a Brahmana.

"O thou of evil understanding, what avails thy
matted hair, what avails thy deer skin? Outwardly
thou cleanest thyself, but within all is darkness."

And later still in the Dhammapada:

"Him I call a Brahmana who, laying aside his
rod, abstains from using it on all creatures, whether
they be moving or still; who neither kills nor incites
others to kill.

"Him I call a Brahmana who knows the mystery
of death and rebirth of all beings, who is free from
attachment, who is happy within himself and enlightened."

Although Buddha, understandably, did not preach against
the caste system—he avoided friction with the society in
which he lived—he made it clear, as we have seen, that he
objected to the concept that it was only by birth that a man
could be a Brahmana, Kshatriya, Vaishya or Sudra. Most of
his followers, throughout the forty-five years during which he
preached his message of the new Arya-Dharma, were Ksha-
triyas and Brahmanas, but Sudras, the caste of menial work-
ers, and even Candalas, outcastes, were admitted as laymem-
bers or as members of his Sangha, or brotherhood of monks.

In the undoubtedly apocryphal *Jātaka* stories there are
about five hundred and fifty tales of the former births,
whether human or animal, of the Buddha, in which he had
been many times a god, a *Brāhman* or a *Kshastriya*.

More than fifteen times he was born in *Brāhman* families,
twice as a *Candāla*, an outcaste, and once into the lowest
caste. He had been born as the king of the monkeys, and, so
the *Jātaka* tales say, as the god Dharma (the Moral Law per-
sonified), as god of the air, as god of the sea, as deity of
trees and as god of the forest, as god of the sacred *Kuśa*

*

grass, and, in two *Jātakas*, he is designated as king of the gods. It was clear how much sacrifice and renunciation a candidate for Buddhahood must make before being reborn as the Buddha in his last birth. There would be no more rebirth. He had reached the sublime goal.

Somewhat later we shall be discussing the role of hypnotism in aiding you to remember earlier lives. At this point let us consider the precedents, Indian and Platonic, for recognizing the act itself as the rediscovery of an ability lost to most men for the better part of the past two thousand years.

The problem is whether we *can* truly remember or more precisely, recollect, this past, or establish the philosophic plausibility of our so doing. To now do so we must however begin with understanding that what we call 'learning' is in actuality 'remembering', and that our 'knowledge' results from our participation in the Omniscience of an imminent spiritual principle, the logical correlative of its timeless omnipresence. To postulate this represents of course a denial of much that we accept as truth in these times, because our way will lie through the now and nowhere of which empirical experience is impossible, even though Memory assures us that this way is open to those who comprehend or understand the Truth.

The Gāyatrī invokes Savitṛ to "impel our intellections" in the *Ṛgveda Samhitā*, and we are told in the *Aitareya Aranyaka* that the self that is in speech is incomplete, since one intuits or senses, when impelled to thought by the Breath (*prāṇena*), not when impelled by speech. (The powers of the soul are called 'selves' in the *Chāndogya Upaniṣad*. In other words, 'the self of speech' means the man considered as a speaker. In this sense, man has as many selves as he has powers.) 'Breath' is to be understood here in its highest sense, that it is not by what we are told, but by the indwelling Spirit that we know and understand the thing to which words can only refer us; that which is sensed does not in itself inform us, but merely provides the occasion and opportunity to recognize the matter to which the external signs have referred us. The Self is necessarily omniscient because it is the only seer, hearer and thinker within us. The empirical self—that with which we are indisputably more familiar—is the instrument of this omniscient Self.

The doctrine is clearly stated in the *Chāndogya Upanisad*, "Memory is from the Self, or Spirit," for the Self knows everything *(Maitri Upanisad)*. Brahma, Self, is intuitive of everything, because, as Sankara says, it is the Self of all *(sarvatman)*, the *only* seer, hearer, thinker, knower and fructuary in us, *(Brhadāranyaka Upanisad)* and therefore, because of Brahma's timeless omnipresence, *must* be omniscient. Memory is a participation in His awareness who never Himself 'remembers' anything, because he never forgets. In other words, as Plotinus says, "Remembering is for those who have forgotten."

As we are told in the *Chāndogya Upanisad*, Memory *(smara)* is more than Space *(ākāśa*, the medium of hearing). Even if many men were to be gathered together, if they were not possessed of Memory, they would neither hear anyone, nor think, nor recognize, but if possessed of Memory they would hear and think and recognize.

The power-of-the-soul that remembers is the Mind *(manas)*, undistracted by the working of the powers of perception and action. There, in what might be described as clairvoyant-sleep *(svapne)*, but which may more correctly be termed the state of contemplation (dhyana), the recognitive person intuits or senses Greatness. Whatever has been seen, he proximately sees; whatever has been heard, he proximately hears. Whatever has been and has not been seen, whatever has been heard and has not been heard, intuitively known or unknown, good or evil, whatever has been directly experienced in any land or air, again and again he directly experiences; he sees it all. *(Prasna Upanisad)* Sankara interprets 'seen and not seen' as referring to what has been seen in this birth and what has been seen in another birth.

The subject of Memory is discussed in the *Milinda Pañha*. It is first shown that it is not by thinking but by Memory that we remember, for we are not without intelligence even when what was done long ago has been forgotten. It is then asked, does Memory arise or come about as an over-knowledge-state * or is Memory factious. The answer is that it is both, and can be either spontaneous or artificially stimulated.

Thus Memory, in the sense that the word is used here, occurs by over-knowledge simply when those who are birth-rememberers remember a birth. It occurs factiously, or needs to be stimulated, when those who are naturally forgetful are stimulated to remember in one or another fashion. In other words, Memory, as Joan Grant has pointed out, is a latent power.

The term birth-rememberers here has to do with the supernormal faculty of remembering past 'dwelling places' possessed by a Buddha or by a highly developed soul, and is distinguished from the memory of a former habitation (or "far-memory," to use Joan Grant's phrase) of those whose memory of the past is included in the factious or stimulated rememberings because means are employed to evoke it.

The supernormal power is exercised at will by a Buddha, and extends to the recollection of any birth whatever, however remote. The brother or student who is not yet a highly developed soul can only, by a step-by-step procedure, recover the memory of one or more births, but no more (*Visuddi Magga*).

Thus what we think we 'learn,' but really 'remember,' suggests that in intuition directly and in learning indirectly we are drawing upon an innate prescience (*prajñāna*). We are told in the *Dīgha Nikāya* that the gods fall from heaven only when their memory fails, and they are of confused memory.** Those whose mind remains uncorrupted, and do not forget,

---

* In Pali Buddhism this generally refers to the supernatural knowledge or omniscience of a Buddha, powers acquired by contemplative discipline by which he or other fully developed souls can intuit at will. There is here a reference to the six powers of levitation (motion at will through the air), clairaudience, thought reading, knowledge of one's own and of other people's birth, and the assurance that the liberation of the soul has been attained.

** For Plato it is a failure to "remember" that drags down from the heights the soul that has walked with God (ie., a *brahmacāiri*) and had some vision of the truths, but cannot retain it.

are immutable and eternal and of a nature that knows no change. Such is the liberated Buddha's prescience or fore-knowing, on which, however, he lays no stress.

It is clearly implied that Memory, as understood here, is a kind of latent knowledge, which may be self-revealed, or may be revived when we are taught (or more correctly *reminded*). There is a clear distinction of mere perception from recognition. Memory is a recovery or re-experiencing, and it may be observed that the other powers which can be experienced at will by the more truly developed are similarly called recoveries. It is evidently not then the outer self, but an inner and immanent power, higher than that of the senses, that remembers or fore-knows by a knowledge that is not easily definable, or as Boethius put it, *unde non PRAEvidentia sed PROvidentia potius dicitur*. That which remembers, or which is always aware of all things, must be a principle always present to all things and therefore itself unaffected by the duration in which these events succeed one another. As Plato wrote in *Phaedrus*, "Every God has an undivided knowledge of things divided and a timeless knowledge of things temporal; he knows the contingent without contingency, the mutable immutably, and in general all things in a higher mode than belongs to their station."

We have thus a Providence (*prajñā*) or Providential Self or Spirit (*prajnatman*) as the ultimate source upon which all Memory draws, and with which whoever attains to the same uninterrupted omniscience must be identified (*Praśna Upanisad*). We have already seen that there is such an omniscient Self, the fount of Memory. It is repeatedly pointed out that this immortal, spiritual fore-knowing Self of all beings, whose presence is undivided in things divided, is our real Self, to be distinguished from the contingent Ego, an apparently unanimous aggregate of powers of perception and action which are only the names of His acts. The providential principle, in other words, is the immanent Spirit, the Knower of the field, apart from whom no birth could take place and apart from whom, as only seer, hearer and thinker in us, neither experience nor memory could be conceived. The verification of the words, "That art thou", must involve at the same time liberation and omniscience.

The connection of omniscience with birth is significant. He who faces all ways and is of many births, he who is the universal life or mover of universal life, and who assumes all forms, is also the All-knower. "Those whose births he knows, they verily come to be *(bhavanti)*, but of those whose births he knoweth not, how might they exist?" *(Aitareya Brāhmana)*. It is the Breath that quickens the emitted semen and knows it, therefore He knows whatever is born *(Satapatha Brāhmana)*. Being omniprogenitive, the Spirit is omnipresent, and being omnipresent it is necessarily omniscient.

This immanent Breath, or 'Life,' is moreover *Vāmadeva*, who says of himself, "Being now (or once for all) in the womb, I have known all the births of the Gods *(Rgveda Samhita)*. Thus spake *Vamadeva*, lying in the womb." * This does not imply a knowledge of successive events, but of all at once, and there is thus established a logical connection of Omniscience, an unbroken Memory of all things, with temporal and spatial Omnipresence. Only from this point of view can the concept of a Providence be made intelligible; the divine life being uneventful inasmuch as all of the events that are for us past and future times are present to it *now*, and not in a succession.

It is at this point that we can turn once more to consider the similar Platonic doctrine, referred to previously, that we do not learn, and that what we call learning is recollection. Plato takes it for granted that the function of works of art is to remind us of the eternal realities, where for those who do not know or contemplate, the remembrance of the heavenly abode is obstructed.**

If we take for granted Plato's repeated distinction of mor-

---

* The doctrine of a knowledge within the womb that is lost at birth, enunciated in the *Garbha Upanisad*, corresponds to the Platonic doctrine that all 'learning' is really recollection.

** In the iconography of Siva, it may be noted, the demon on whom he tramples is called "the person of amnesia."

tal and immortal 'souls' that dwell together in us (calling to mind Dr. Denys Kelsey's statement that it is unusual to find an individual in whom several supra-physicals do not co-exist), and assuming further that the immortal is not an individual but a universal principle participated in by the individual, we then recognize that the Soul of Man is immortal, and at one time reaches a nominal end which is called 'dying', and is then born again. Since then this Soul is immortal and has been born many times, and has beheld all things both in this world and in what we term Hades, this soul has learnt all things, without exception, and should be able to remember all that he knew before, about virtue and other things.

In Rumi's *Mathnawi* we find the concept also found in the Qur'an (6.80): "What wonder then if the spirit does not remember its ancient abodes, which have been its dwelling place and birthplace aforetime, since this world, like sleep, is covering it over as clouds cover the stars? Especially as it has trodden so many cities, and the dust has not yet been swept from its perceptive faculty, nor has it made ardent efforts that its heart should become pure and behold the past; that its heart should put forth its head from the aperture of the mystery and should see the beginning and the end with open eye." The doctrine that God is the real agent and man only his instrument is also found in the *Mantiqu't-Tair*:

"All you have been, and seen, and done, and thought.
Not *you*, but *I*, have seen and been and wrought."

We could not possibly have learned in some prior time what we now remember if the Soul in us had not existed anywhere before being born in this human nature. The Soul knows things of which we could not have acquired any knowledge in this life and must, as Socrates points out, have had this learning through all time.

Plato's Immortal Soul, "the most lordly and divine part of us", is the *Sanctus Spiritus* as distinguished from the (mortal) soul (*Hebrews 4.12*), and St. Ambrose's "source of all that is true, by whomsoever it has been said", cited by St.

Thomas Aquinas, Dante's Amor, and Meister Eckhart's "as a clear mirror sees all things in one image." In the Talmud (Nidda 30 B) and in the Zohar (Wayyiqra, Aharei Mot), we are told that all human souls have a full knowledge of the Torah and retain all their knowledge until they come down to earth and are born. Manasseh Ben Israel, writing in the 17th century, saw here the equivalent of Plato's doctrine of Recollection, for it must follow that whatever is learnt after birth can only amount to a recovery of this knowledge. The doctrine survives in Blake's, "Is the Holy Ghost any other than an intellectual fountain?"

There is no need to here follow up the history of the doctrine of Recollection in greater detail. The importance and universality of the doctrine is as obvious as is its relevance to the concept with which we are concerned in this book. It is clear that this is one of the many consistent features of a philosophy, a perennial philosophy if we may so term it, which is essentially the same in Plato as in the Vedas.

III

ISLAM AND THE SOUL

Say, He alone is God: God the Eternal. He begetteth not, and He is not begotten; there is none like unto Him. Praise be to God, the Lord of the worlds, the Compassionate, the Merciful, King on the day of reckoning; Thee only do we worship, and to Thee do we cry for help. Guide us on the straight path, the path of those to whom Thou art gracious, with whom Thou art not angry; such as go not astray.*

. . . . With Him are the keys of the unseen. None knows them save He; He knows what is in the land and in the sea; no leaf falleth but He knoweth it; nor is there a grain in the darkness under the earth, nor a thing, green or sere, but it is recorded by itself. He taketh your souls in the night, and knoweth what the work of your day deserveth; then He awaketh you, that the set life-term may be fulfilled; then unto Him shall ye return, and then shall He declare unto you what you have wrought.**

When the sun shall be folded up, and the stars shall fall, and when the mountains shall be set in motion; when the she-camels shall be left, and the wild beasts shall be gathered together; when the seas shall boil, and souls be re-paired ***; when the

* Surat-ul-Fâtiha, the opening chapter of the Koran.
** Sura, vi. 59, 60.
*** i.e., with their bodies.

female child that was buried alive shall be asked
for what crime she was put to death; when the
leaves of the Book shall be unrolled, and the heavens shall be stripped away, and the fire of hell blaze
forth, and paradise draw nigh, then shall every soul
know what it hath done.*

Notwithstanding the implication of the above, Islam's approach to the idea of a future existence—of an existence after
the separation of the living principle of our nature from the
mortal part, is perhaps more accurately reflected, as far as
most people are concerned, by still another passage in the
Koran:**

"O thou soul which art at rest, return unto thy
Lord, pleased and pleasing him, enter thou among
my servants, and enter thou my garden of felicity."

Except in metaphysically minded circles, influenced as
much by Neo-Platonist teachings as by indigenous philosophic
traditions, there has been comparatively little interest in this
aspect of what has been termed the Inner meaning of the
Koran. Throughout the early years of Islam, through to perhaps the 13th century, this interest in the Inner meaning beyond the allegories of the revelations is one of the most fascinating aspects of life in this period of Islam's undisputed political and cultural greatness.

It must be kept in mind that then, as now, Islam was a
world community. Teachers from Seville and Cordova taught
in Baghdad or Damascus. There was an exchange of opinions
between east and west, and a degree of intellectual ferment
and independent speculative thought far more alive, and
impressive, than is conceivable in these days, the at times di-
vergent schools of thought reflecting the catholicity (if we
may use the expression) that is Islam.

What we have to keep in mind however is that the belief
of Jew, Zoroastrian, and Christian in a bodily resurrection is

* Sura lxxxi.
** Sura lxxxix, 27–30 (Koran and Quran are used interchangeably).

not what concerns us in the present study. Primitive Christianity, with its vivid belief in the imminent advent of the material kingdom of Christ, influenced by Chaldean, Mago-Zoroastrian, and Alexandrian schools of thought, represented a concern with material rewards and punishments in a future existence, not a rebirth.

Similarly, the chief and predominating idea in Islam about a future life is predicated upon the belief that, in a state of existence in a hereafter, every human being will have to render an account of his actions on earth, and the happiness or misery of individuals will depend upon the manner in which he can be said to have performed the behests of his Creator. The Creator's mercy and grace are nevertheless unbounded and will thus be bestowed alike upon His creatures. This is the pivot on which the whole doctrine of future life in Islam turns, and this is the only doctrinal point a Muslim is required to believe and accept. Quasi-schismatic approaches, such as those which will concern us shortly, reflecting the floating traditions of the races and peoples of the time, are thus dismissed with varying degrees of grace as philosophic accessories. Ignoring for the moment the question of the subjectivity involved in the cited ideas of future rewards and punishments, the orthodox agree that in all ideas of a life-after-death (as distinct from what we are concerned with), these ideas have furnished to the moral teachers of the world the most powerful instrument for influencing the conduct of individuals and nations. In marked contrast to the Buddhist approach, this has however been expressed in the form of moral prohibitions, sanctions, if you wish, which demand obedience rather than understanding. As far as the orthodox are concerned, it is conceded that philosophy has wrangled over abstract expressions, which obviously could not be easily understood by the layman. These expressions and these conceptions have seen their day, points out the traditionalist, have flourished, and have died without making themselves felt beyond a restricted circle of dreamers who it is held lived in the indefinable vagueness of their own thoughts.

Thus the traditionalist within Islam, as within Christianity, is not concerned so much with the revelation as with the *interpretation* of the revelation which, ignoring metaphysical subtleties, is more concerned with the tangible than with the intangible. (It is, as a matter of fact, only in the last generations, particularly in what is now Pakistan, that there has been a revival of interest in speculative as distinct from traditionalist thought.) Thus while many within Islam feel that, after physical death, the individual soul "returns" to the Universal Soul and that the joys and the pains spoken of by the teachers are mental and subjective, most believe in the literal fulfillment of all the word-paintings of the Koran.

For instance, when Mohammed talked of the excesses men committed to the injury of their own souls, the orthodox interpreted this literally, very much as the Calvinists in their day would interpret the Bible, while the dreamers, if we may so term them, extrapolated from the tangible to the less tangible. Let us therefore turn to these dreamers.

But before we do so let us remember that the subtleties of these so-called dreamers, apart from the fact that they reflect the theistic diversities possible within Islam, to some extent also reflect the influence upon these intellectuals of indigenous philosophic traditions.

Therefore when we talk of Persian metaphysics, and of Sufism, we are concerned with philosophic abstractions reflecting the Persian temperament and the reality that in Persia philosophical speculation has indissolubly associated itself with religion, since long before the Arab conquest, and thinkers in new lines of thought have almost always been founders of new religious movements, with rare exceptions within Islam.

The Zoroastrian view of the destiny of the soul had been that the soul was a creation, not a part of God, as the votaries of Mithra afterwards maintained.* The soul had a beginning in time but could attain to everlasting life by fighting

---

* Mithraists worshipped the sun, looking upon it as the great advocate of Light. The human soul was a part of God; the soul's union with God was thus possible after it had passed through the sphere of Ether and become pure fire.

against evil in the earthly scene of its activity. It was free to choose between the only two courses of action—good and evil, but, in addition to this power of choice, the spirit of Light had endowed it with the following faculties: Conscience, Vital force, The Soul—The Mind, The Spirit—Reason, and the *Farawashi*, tutelary spirits which acted as the protection of man in his voyage towards God.

The last three faculties were united together after death, and formed an indissoluble whole. The virtuous soul, leaving its home of flesh, was borne up into higher regions, and had to pass through the following planes of existence:

(1) The Place of good thoughts

(2) The Place of good words

(3) The Place of good works

(4) The Place of Eternal Glory, where the individual soul would unite with the principle of Light without losing its personality.

The Sufi conception of the soul is likewise tripartite. According to it the soul is a combination of Mind, Heart and Spirit, with Heart understood to be both material and immaterial. The Sufi cosmology has a similar doctrine concerning the different stages of existence through which the soul has to pass in its journey heavenward. They enumerate the following five Planes:

(1) The world of body

(2) The world of pure intelligence

(3) The world of power

(4) The world of negation

(5) The world of Absolute Silence.

The more materialistic cosmology of Mani, who was born in Babylonia about 215 A.D. at a time when Buddhist missionaries were beginning to preach Nirvana to the Persians, represented an extension of the Christian idea of redemption. Mani taught that a variety of things sprang from the mixture of two eternal Principles—Light and Darkness—which were separate from and independent of each other. The Principle of Light connoted ten ideas: gentleness, knowledge, understanding, mystery, insight, love, conviction, faith, benevolence and wisdom, while the Principle of Darkness connoted five eternal ideas: mistiness, heat, fire, venom, darkness. Mani recognized the eternity of space and earth, each connoting respectively the ideas of knowledge, understanding, mystery, insight, breath, air, water, light and fire.

It is worth noting that Mani was the first to suggest that the Universe was due to the activity of the Devil, and hence essentially evil, a logical justification for a system which preached renunciation as the guiding principle of life, much as Schopenhauer later was to do. The subsequent doctrinal controversy among the Zoroastrians indicates a movement towards a monistic conception of the universe, but there is relatively little evidence of pantheistic tendencies in pre-Islamic Persian thought. We know that in the sixth century, Diogenes, Simplicius, and other Neo-Platonists, were driven by Justinian's persecution to take refuge at the Persian court. A number of works were translated for the Persian monarch from Sanskrit and Greek, but we have no historical evidence of the possible influence of this on pre-Arab Persian thought.

A new era was to begin with the Arab conquest of the country. It was the beginning of interaction between Aryan and Semitic cultures, but while the Persian let the surface of his life become largely Semiticised, he quietly converted Islam, and not necessarily only within the borders of the country, to his own Aryan habits of thought. There is a marked transition from the purely objective attitude of pre-Islamic Persian philosophy to the subjective attitude of later thinkers. The combination of the subtle Persian intellect, and the increased interest in Greek thought, resulted in the development of a hybrid Persian Neo-Platonism, representing an effort at the discovery rather than exposition of the philosophies of Aristotle and Plato.

Abu 'Ali Muhammad ibn Muhammad ibn Ya'qub, commonly known as Ibn Maskawaih (d. 1030 A.D.), the treasurer of the Buwaihid Sultan 'Adaduddaula, is recognized as one of the most eminent theistic thinkers, physicians, moralists and historians of Persia. Ibn Maskawaih, having shown that the soul could not be regarded as a function of matter, proceeded to establish that it was essentially immaterial.

The soul could conceive certain propositions that had no connection with the sense-data. The senses, for instance, could not perceive that two contradictories could not exist together.

There was a certain power in us which ruled over physical organs, corrected sense-errors, and unified all knowledge. This unifying principle which reflected over the material brought before it through the sense-channel and, weighing the evidence of each sense, decided the character of rival statements, must itself stand above the sphere of matter.

The combined force of these and other considerations established the truth of the proposition that the soul was essentially immaterial. The immateriality of the soul signified its immortality, since mortality was a characteristic of the material.

The physician Avicenna (d. 1037 A.D.) was specially interested in the nature of the Soul. In his time the doctrine of Metempsychosis was becoming more and more popular. Avicenna discussed the nature of the soul with a view to showing the falsity of the doctrine, beginning with the assertion that it was difficult to define the soul since it manifested different powers and tendencies in different planes of being. He argued that the doctrine of Metempsychosis implied individual pre-existence. Assuming that the soul did exist before the body, it must have existed either as one or as many. The multiplicity of bodies was due to the multiplicity of material forms and did not indicate the multiplicity of souls. Body and soul were contiguous to each other, but quite opposite in their respective essences.

It is interesting to note however that he felt that the disintegration of the body did not necessitate the annihilation of the soul. Dissolution or decay was a property of compounds and not of simple, indivisible, ideal substances. While he thus denied pre-existence, he did recognize the possibility of disembodied conscious life beyond the grave.

The orthodox reaction against rationalism, represented by

the ninth century Ash'arite school represented a defense of the authority of Divine Revelation. It was an attempt not only to purge Islam of all non-Islamic elements which had quietly crept into it, but also to harmonize the religious consciousness with the religious thought of Islam.

Rationalism was an attempt to measure reality by reason alone; implying the identity of the spheres of religion and philosophy, it strove to express faith in the form of concepts or pure thought. It in short ignored the facts of human nature.

In opposition to the Rationalists the Ash'arites maintained the doctrine of the Attributes of God. God, according to the Ash'arite, was the ultimate necessary existence which carried its attributes in its own being, and whose existence and essence were identical. An interesting aspect of Ash'arite metaphysics is their rejection of the idea of causation. The orthodox believed in miracles as well as in the Universal Law of Causation; at the time of manifesting a miracle, God would suspend the operation of this law. The Ash'arite, starting with the supposition that cause and effect must be similar, taught that the idea of power was meaningless, and that we knew nothing but floating impressions, the phenomenal order of which was determined by God.

Any account, even as cursory as this, of Ash'arite metaphysics, would be incomplete without mention of the work of Al-Ghazali (d. 1111 A.D.), a sceptic of powerful ability who has been said to have anticipated Descartes in his philosophical method. He was the first to write a systematic refutation of philosophy, and completely to annihilate that dread of intellectualism which had characterized the orthodox. It was chiefly due to his influence that men began to study dogma *and* metaphysics.

The soul, according to Al-Ghazali, perceives things. But perception as an attribute can exist only in a substance or essence which is absolutely free from all the attributes of body. He explained why the Prophet Mohammed declined to reveal the true nature of the soul. There were two kinds of men, ordinary men and thinkers. The former, who looked upon materiality as a condition of existence, could not conceive of an immaterial substance. The latter were led by their logic to a conception of the soul that swept away all difference between God and the individual soul. Al-Ghazali therefore preferred silence to explaining the ultimate nature of the soul.

An important theological effect of the Ash'arite philosophy was that it checked the growth of free thought within Islam. It led also to an independent criticism of Greek philosophy.

The Ash'arite denial of Aristotle's Prima Materia, and their views concerning the nature of space, time and causation, however, awakened that irrepressible spirit of controversy which, for centuries, in a sense divided Islam. A number of factors, political, social, and intellectual, contributed to the almost simultaneous coming into existence of the Sufi ideal of life—a reaction to the unsettled times; the sceptical tendencies of Islamic rationalism; the unemotional piety of the various schools of Islam—the Hanafite, the Malikite, and the anthropomorphic Hambalite school, the bitterest enemy of independent thought; the bitter theological controversy between the Ash'arites and the advocates of Rationalism; the gradual softening of religious fervency at one period and the rapid growth of wealth which tended to produce moral laxity and indifference to religious life in the upper circles of Islam; and the presence of Christianity as a working ideal of life, though more the actual life of the Christian hermit than his religious ideas. There is as a matter of fact a remarkable similarity between the conditions which Neo-Platonism represented a reaction to, and these conditions, six hundred years later, which contributed to the development of Sufism.

The extraordinary vitality of the Sufi restatement of Islam is explained when we consider the all-embracing nature of Sufism. The Sufi message to the individual is, "Love all, and forge your own individuality in doing good to others." Or, as Jalalu'd'din Rumi (1207–1273) put it: "To win other people's hearts is the greatest pilgrimage; and one heart is worth more than a thousand Ka'bas. Ka'ba is a mere cottage of Abraham; but the heart is the very home of God."

Of more interest to us, perhaps, is his poem:

"I died as mineral and became a plant,
I died as plant and rose to animal,
I died as animal and I was Man.
Why should I fear? When was I less by dying?
Yet once more I shall die as Man, to soar
With angels blest; but even from angelhood
I must pass on. . . ."

The Sufis justify their views from the Koranic standpoint. They contend that the Prophet had an esoteric teaching—"wisdom", as distinguished from the teachings contained in the Book, and cite Sura 2, v. 14: "As we have sent a prophet to you from among yourselves who reads our verses to you, purifies you, teaches you the Book and the Wisdom, and teaches you what you did not know before." The Sufi contends that the Wisdom spoken of in the verse is something not incorporated in the teachings of the Book which, as the Prophet repeatedly declared, had been taught by several prophets before him.

The Koran defines the Muslims as, "Those who believe in the Unseen, establish daily prayer, and spend out of what We have given them." *

The question now arises as to the *what* and the *where* of the Unseen.

The Koran replies that the Unseen is in your own soul, "And in the earth there are signs to those who believe, and in yourself—what! do you not then see!" ** Similarly the Holy Book teaches that the essential nature of the Unseen is pure light, "God is the light of heavens and earth." *** As for whether the Primal Light is personal, the Koran, in spite of many expressions signifying personality, declares,—"There is nothing like him." ****

Sufi commentators enumerate four stages of spiritual training through which the soul—the order or reason of the

* Sura 2, v. 2
** Sura 51, v. 20, 21
*** Sura 24, v. 35
**** Sura 42, v. 9

Primal Light—must pass, if it desires to rise above the mass, and realize its union or identity with the ultimate source of all things. These stages are:

(1) Belief in the Unseen

(2) Search after the Unseen

(3) The knowledge of the Unseen, by looking into the depths of our own soul

(4) The Realisation, resulting from the constant practise of Justice and Charity. "Verily God bids you do justice and good, and give to kindred, and He forbids you to sin, and do wrong, and oppress." *

The Ishraqi school of thought is distinguished by its intellectual independence and by its faithfulness to the philosophic traditions of the country. The young Shaikh Shahabal Din Suhrawardi, known as Shaikhal Ishraq Maqtul, murdered on the order of Sultan Salah-al Din late in the 12th century, differed in many fundamental points from Plato and freely criticised Aristotle. He maintained that the student, if he was to fully comprehend the purely intellectual side of Transcendental Philosophy, must be thoroughly acquainted with Aristotelian Philosophy, Logic, Mathematics, and Sufism. His mind should be completely free from the taint of prejudice and sin, so that he might gradually develop that inner sense which verifies and corrects what intellect only understands as theory. Unaided reason was untrustworthy; it must always be supplemented by the perception of the essence of things which brings knowledge and peace to the restless soul, and disarms scepticism forever.

He taught that man as an active being had the following motive powers:

(a) Reason or the Angelic soul—the source of intelligence, discrimination, and love of knowledge

(b) The beast-soul—the source of anger, courage, dominance, and ambition

(c) The animal soul—the source of lust, hunger and sexual passion.

* Sura 16, v. 92.

The first led to wisdom; the second and third, if controlled by reason, led respectively to bravery and chastity. The harmonious use of all resulted in the virtue of justice. It was by the union of knowledge and virtue that the soul would free itself from the world of darkness.

Let us finally consider Shaikh al Akbar Muhiyiddin Ibn al Arabi (1164–1240), the Spanish-born Sufi philosopher and poet. Ibn 'Arabi is said to have exercised a considerable influence, through his writings, on both Dante and upon Raymond Lully, the Spanish mystic.

While still a young man he had begun to show signs of prophetic greatness. A clairvoyant and a telepath, he would at times go into a prophetic trance. In 1202 he left Seville for the East, at first only with the intention of performing the pilgrimage to Mecca, but he never returned to Spain. The story is told of the conversation when he first met the man who was to become his best known disciple, and who asked him, "Whence do you come? Whither would you go? What have you to obtain on the road?" Ibn 'Arabi's answer was quick: "From knowledge to the substance, to attain both the ends."

By 1214 when he returned to Mecca for the second time (he had by then lived there for seven years after which he had traveled throughout Mesopotamia and Syria), the Shaikh was considered to be the most prominent living saint in the Hejaz and in Syria. Scholars of note and Sufis of great repute came to visit him from abroad to have his blessings and, as it was put, to learn from him the truths of the upper world and the realities of this lower one. He became famous as a Sufi of high order, a composer of elegant mystic verses, and a writer of immense volumes * on the most abstruse and difficult subjects. He had an great following and was admired by most people for his toleration,** his catholic outlook on life, his piety and scholarship and insight into the realities of existence. A conformist in religion, an esotericist in his inner be-

---

* he was the author of nearly three hundred works.
** the different religions were equivalent in his opinion.

liefs, his sole guide was the inner light with which he believed himself illuminated in a special way.

One of his earlier works is *Al Futuhat al Makkiyya*, begun in Mecca in 1204. He writes in the introduction:

> "As I was writing this introduction, I saw through illumination Muhammad in the world of Real Ideas near the Great Presence. When I saw him there as the chief, he welcomed me and said, 'Here is a quality common to both of us!' Then a pulpit was ordered for in that aweful place. On the top of the pulpit was written: 'This is the sacred place of Muhammad, he who mounted it inherited the custody of truths and realities and became the guardian of the Shari'at.'
>
> "At that place I was given all wisdom and endowed with concise speaking. I thanked God and mounted the pulpit till I reached the place of Muhammad. Several pieces of white cloth were placed on the place touched by Muhammad's feet, so that my feet might not touch that sacred place."

Then the Shaikh gives a long conversation between him and the Prophet.

Once, while walking around the Ka'ba, he met a celestial spirit in the form of a youth engaged in the same rite, who showed him the living esoteric temple concealed under the apparently lifeless exterior. When he had recovered—he had fainted from shock—Ibn al 'Arabi entered the Ka'ba with the young man who, resuming his spiritual aspect, appeared to him on a three-legged horse. The youth then breathed into the breast of Ibn al 'Arabi the knowledge of all things and once more ordered him to describe the heavenly form in which all mysteries are enshrined.

He claimed that every word of *Al Futuhat al Makkiyya* (or "Meccan Revelations") was dictated to him by supernatural means. With this in mind it is interesting that at one point he should write in this work:

"*Nubuwat* is information to souls,
Confined by bodies having souls"

And elsewhere, in the same work:

"There is some difference of opinion among the
Muslim learned men as regards the method of Resurrection. Some of them say that Resurrection will
be by reincarnation and quote passages from the
Quran and authenticated sayings of the Prophet in
support of their contention."

In the *Fusūs al Hikam* he wrote:

"God's knowledge of essence is His knowledge of
all individual souls. The soul, as a mode of Divine
being, determines its own destiny. Everyone's por-
tion in this world is that which God knows he will
receive and which is all that he is capable of receiv-
ing. God Himself cannot alter it."

In *Al Fas al Shēthiyyah*, perhaps on an autobiographical
note, he was to write:

"When a man of illumination sees a figure which
gives instructions in matters that he did not know
before, that figure is from his own self proper. It is
just like the figure in the mirror, which appears
oblong or round, long or short, according to the
character of the mirror."

And on this same note, let us end this much too brief discussion of the Islamic approach to this question of what the
Soul is. In *Al Fas al Adamiyyah* the Shaikh wrote:

"Angels are the powers hidden in the faculties and
organs of man."

IV

WHO ELSE BELIEVED— AND BELIEVES?

In the next pages we will be concerned, much too briefly, with the views of those who have believed, or still believe, in the concept of Reincarnation, beginning with the approach of the Greeks to this subject.

I am the first to admit that any discussion of the Greek understanding of the Mysteries, within the confines of a few pages, is close to being an impossibility.

But this book is primarily intended for the general reader, for whom even the word Mysteries has a bacchic rather than metaphysical connotation. Within the limitations imposed upon us we must therefore, in this bird's eye view, if it may be phrased this way, attempt to introduce you briefly to the world of the Greek and the Romans, after which we will touch on the world of the Medicis and of Dante, and of Wagner, before turning to relatively contemporary interest in and acceptance of the concept, attempting, here and there, in passing, to correct some misunderstandings, born in part out of our fundamental inability to understand those who have gone before us, except in terms of reference translatable in our values.

Orpheus, who may not, for that matter, have been a Greek (his name suggests that he was dark complexioned), is the Thracian singer who was initiated both into the Egyptian Mysteries, from which he secured extensive knowledge of magic, astrology, sorcery and medicine, and into the Mysteries of the Cabiri at Samothrace, adding to his knowledge of medicine and music.

While undoubtedly *a* founder (if not *the* founder) of the

Greek mythological system, which he used as the medium for the promulgation of his philosophical doctrines, Orpheus was in time to become the symbol of the Greek school of the ancient wisdom. We are told in Plato's *Republic* that the soul that had once been Orpheus, facing the time when it must live again in the physical world, chose rather to return in the body of a swan than to be born of a woman. This allegory of Orpheus incarnating in the white swan—the swan is the symbol of the initiates of the Mysteries—has been held to mean that the spiritual truths he promulgated would continue and would be taught by the illumined initiates of future ages.

The cult which developed around what are termed the Orphic Mysteries taught that the soul was divine, immortal, and aspired to freedom, while the body held it in fetters as a prisoner. Death dissolved the bondage but only to reimprison the liberated soul after a short time, since the wheel of birth revolved inexorably.

This was to some extent a departure from the older Cult of Souls we know from the Homeric poems. Homer consistently assumes the departure of the soul, through the mouth or through an open wound, into an inaccessible land of the dead where it exists in an unconscious half-life. The ceremonial burning of the dead warrior, often in the company of captives taken in the recent battle, the details resembling the obsequies for Viking chiefs close to two thousand years later, were in part a gesture of respect but also prompted by the certainty that cremation prevented the return of the dead to the old surroundings.

In later days it was commonly assumed that the dead, invisible, were all around you. They were not necessarily bound to the immediate neighborhood of the grave—pictures on Attic oil flasks show their winged figures, diminutive in size, hovering over the grave-monument—they would often revisit their old home. There was the popular habit of letting anything that fell to the ground remain there for the spirits hovering about the house to carry away if they so chose. With this in mind one obviously did not speak ill of the dead, lest the "Blessed Ones", as the dead were being called even in the fifth century, might be displeased.

In the Eleusianian Mysteries it was likewise felt that birth into the physical world was death in the fullest sense of the word, and that the only true birth was that of the spiritual soul of man rising out of the womb of his own fleshly nature. It was felt that man, accepting as his real self the senseless clay that he'd see reflected in a mirror or in the water, lost the opportunity afforded by his present physical life to unfold or to develop his immortal, invisible Self.

It has been said that "the living are ruled by the dead." This was true in a sense, as we've seen, in Solon's Athens. Those familiar with the Eleusinian concept of life will recognize however that this means that the majority of people are not ruled by their living spirits but by their senseless and hence "dead" animal personalities. Transmigration and Reincarnation were taught in the Eleusinian Mysteries, but not quite in the way we might expect. It was believed that at midnight the invisible worlds were closest to the worlds known to the physically living and that souls coming into material existence would slip in during this midnight hour. Many of the ceremonies were thus performed at midnight, at which time those spirits who had failed to awaken their higher natures during their prior lives and were therefore condemned to existence in an outer darkness might slip through at this hour and assume (or enter into) forms of various creatures.

The Mysteries survived long into the first centuries of the Christian era, until their suppression by Emperor Theodosius, four hundred years after the birth of Christ. Their influence had lessened by then—other schools of thought had come to the forefront—but it is worth noting that Pindar, Plato, Cicero and Epictetus, at one or another time, spoke of them with admiration, Cicero saying, characteristically, that the Mysteries taught men not only how to live but also how to die.

In other words, the Greeks had Mystery traditions ante-dating those taught by the homeless Greek philosophers, slaves in some instances, who taught their Roman conquerors and were acknowledged by these Romans to be the only truly civilized people. There is reason to believe that more than one Greek smiled inwardly at hearing this.

Pythagoras, the son of Mnesarchus, who lived in the sixth century before Christ, came before these bitter men however.

We are told that, after having become an initiate in the Eleusinian Mysteries, he went to Egypt, and was finally initiated in the Mysteries of Isis at the hands of the priests at Thebes. Then he traveled to Syria, where the Mysteries of Adonis were conferred upon him, studied with the surviving Chaldeans and then, for several years, under the teachers at Elephanta and Ellora. He appears to have been known there as *Yavancharya*, or the Greek teacher.

After his return from his wanderings Pythagoras, who preferred to describe himself as a philosopher—"one who is attempting to find out", instead of as a sage, generally accepted to mean, "those who know"—established a school at Crotona, a Dorian colony in Southern Italy.

The teachings of Pythagoras, who was assassinated in 507 B.C. (one is tempted to add, "of course"), were the fruit of his contact with the leading philosophers of the entire civilized world of his day. The study of geometry, music and astronomy was considered essential to a rational understanding of God, man or Nature, and no one could study under Pythagoras as a disciple who was not thoroughly familiar with these sciences.

The God of Pythagoras was the *Monad*, or the One that is Everything. He described God as the Supreme Mind distributed throughout all parts of the universe—the Cause of all things, the Intelligence of all things, and the Power within all things. He declared the motion of this God to be circular, the body of God to be composed of the substance of light, and the nature of God to be composed of the substance of truth.

He taught that both man and the universe were made in the image of God; that both being made in the same image, the understanding of one predicted the knowledge of the other. He further taught that there was a constant interplay between the Grand Man (the universe) and man (the little universe).

He has been described as teaching that human souls could incarnate in animal forms—that mortals who during their earthly existence had behaved like certain animals would return to earth again in the form of these animals whom they had resembled in their earlier life. This conflicts, however, with what we may term as the Pythagorean scheme, and it is far more likely that he was speaking allegorically, intending to convey the idea that humans become bestial when they allow themselves to be dominated by their lower desires and destructive tendencies.*

Pythagoras accepted the concept of successive reappearances of the spiritual nature in human form. He himself, he said, had been Aethalides, a son of Mercury; Euphorbos, son of Panthus, killed by Menelaus at the siege of Troy; Hermothimus, a prophet of Clazomenae, a city of Ionia; a humble fisherman; and finally the philosopher of Samos. He had received as a gift from Mercury the memory of his soul's transmigrations, and also the gift of remembering what his own soul, and the souls of others, had experienced between death and rebirth.

We are told Plato's real name was Aristocles, and that when his father brought him to study with Socrates, the great philosopher declared that on the previous night he had dreamt about a white swan, an omen that his new disciple was to become one of the world's few illumined ones. Plato, like Pythagoras, had traveled widely, and had studied Hermetic philosophy in Egypt. He was also influenced by the Pythagoreans.

The Platonic discipline was founded upon the theory that learning is really reminiscence, or the bringing into objectiv-

---

* Hierocles, a Pythagorean, wrote that he who believed that the soul transmigrated, after death, into the body of a beast or plant, was grossly mistaken, and was ignorant of the fact that the essential form of soul could not change, it was and remained human. Only metaphorically speaking could virtue make of it a god, or vice transform it into an animal.

ity of knowledge acquired by the soul in a previous state of existence. As far as he was concerned, every soul was immortal, "for whatever is in perpetual motion *is* immortal."

Plato himself recognized Aristotle (384–322 B.C.) as his greatest disciple. But, though Aristotle did talk of the soul as immortal, we have no reason to believe that he fully accepted the concept of the pre-existence of the soul. To Aristotle the soul was that by which man first lived, felt, and understood. He assigned three faculties to the soul: nutritive, sensitive, and intellective. He further considered the soul to be twofold —rational and irrational—and in some particulars elevated the sense perceptions above the mind.

Apollonius of Tyana was a leading personality of the Neo-Pythagorean school that flourished in Alexandria during the first century of the Christian Era, and represented a link between the older philosophies and Neo-Platonism. Like the latter, the school emphasized metaphysical speculation and ascetic habits.

This seer (for it was proven that he had unusual powers) is quoted as saying, "There is no death of anything save in appearance." When he wrote this he may have been thinking of the time when he had been initiated into the Mysteries, allegedly in the Great Pyramid, and was, as a part of the ritual, left hanging upon a cross until unconscious and then laid in a tomb for three days. While he was unconscious, it was thought that his soul had passed into the realms of the immortals, the place of death. After the soul had conquered death, by recognizing that life is eternal, the soul returned again to the body which rose from its coffin, upon which he was hailed as a brother by the priests who believed that he had returned from the land of the dead.

Ammonius Saccus was the founder, in A.D. 193, of the famous Alexandrian School of Neo-Platonism, the Philathelians, or the "lovers of truth". His disciples included Origen, Plotinus, Philo Judaeus, Iamblichus and the Emperor Julian.

Just as much as there is an interesting similarity between Neo-Pythagoreanism and the doctrines of the Essenes, we find many of the basic tenets of Neo-Platonism accepted, despite their "pagan" origin, and being woven into the fabric of what we term Patristic philosophy, that is, the philosophy of the Fathers of the Early Christian Church. Something about Alexandria, perhaps its incomparable library, perhaps the welcome accorded scholars from abroad (at this time, of course), made not for ecumenicism, but for a kind of co-existence.

Neo-Platonism was concerned almost exclusively with the problems of higher metaphysics. It recognized the existence of a secret doctrine which, from the beginning of known history, had been concealed within the rituals, symbols and allegories of religions and philosophies.

When the physical body of so-called pagan thought collapsed, an attempt was made to resurrect the form by instilling new life into it by the unveiling of its mystical truths.

It was too late. Platonism, or more precisely Neo-Platonism, was to be nearly forgotten for the better part of a thousand years. Plotinus (205–270), Iamblichus, who died about 333, and Hypatia, the Neo-Platonic philosopher and mathematician, who was murdered by a Christian mob in 415, each accepted the concept of pre-existence. With Hypatia's death fell the Neo-Platonic School of Alexandria. Cyril, Bishop of Alexandria, and later to be canonized for his zeal, did not believe in co-existence.

Individual Greek philosophers, at the Roman court and elsewhere, kept the doctrine alive. But interest was limited to the romantics and to the schismatics. The world was a wonderful place to live in. Never mind the storm warnings. Never mind the obvious breakdown of the so-called Roman way of life. As in more recent times, people obviously did not care if there ever would be a tomorrow.

In any approach to the world of the Romans and to what they thought, we must forget every play by William Shakespeare that we may ever have seen.

We must instead keep in mind the reality that, apart from the fact that we are talking about the few, the term itself is a loose one, political rather than ethnic, and has to do more with people subject to the laws of Rome by reason of their being tax-paying citizens or officials than to the possibility that they were in fact Roman-born. Neither emperor nor citizen would normally be born in Rome, except in the case of the poor, and they did not count.

Rome was a cosmopolitan city in the days of the Empire —very much as New York and London are today—more so, certainly, than during the Renaissance—and very much the center of the world as far as its merchants and leading citizens and poets and litterateurs were concerned.

As lawless as our cities are today, Rome also had her slums, festering sprawling rabbit warrens in which tens of thousands lived out their lives, unable to escape this existence except by dying or by selling themselves, or their young, into lifelong servitude on the land.

Rome also had her temples and her public buildings and her palaces, the temples dedicated to the many gods who had in a sense come under the Roman aegis, the public buildings and the palaces crowded with those who, by reason of birth or of innate ability, as much the one as the other, belonged to the Establishment of the day.

Yes, Rome was a cosmopolitan city—its streets crowded with peoples from all over the world, from the Levant or from North Africa, from Gaul or from Cappadocia—the temples to the foreign gods outnumbering the temples dedicated to those gods to whom Romans had prayed before Constantine, for various and sundry practical reasons, had turned his back, at least publicly, on that past.

By the close of the fourth century, the majority of the Senate were still not Christians, although the wives and daughters of some had accepted Christianity in its most ascetic form. The officials were usually nominal Christians—it was the Court religion, after all—but nobody, least of all the urbane and sophisticated clerics surrounding the Bishops of Rome, rhetoricians rather than men of faith, troubled to look too closely into this matter.

The shrines of the gods still surrounded the imperial palace in all their old splendor and, as late as half-way through the fifth century, a prefect of Rome could ridicule the Christians, quarrelling over doctrinal minutiae, who obviously did not understand that their faith was doomed, and rejoice, in the same breath, at the sight of villagers in Etruria gaily celebrating the rites of Osiris in the springtime.

Christianity was indeed far from triumphant. Indeed, though magic and divination had long been banned by the state, a prefect of Honorius (395–423 A.D.) could still propose the use of Tuscan sorcerers who had volunteered their services against Alaric, King of the Visigoths. In the last years of the Western Empire the diviners of Africa were practising their arts among the nominal Christians of Aquitaine.

As a matter of fact, many noble poets in Aquitaine were fully as pagan as the peasant who bowed before the old altars. His grandfather might have conformed to Christianity, and some of his friends might have followed Saint Jerome to Jerusalem, but he himself was as little a Christian as those who, not too many years before him, had petitioned the Emperor to leave the Altar of Victory in the Senate chamber. He might pay a cold and perfunctory homage to Christ, in whose name the Emperor in far off Rome still ruled, and visit the neighboring town for the Easter festival, but his thought and his life were inspired and influenced by the past. All the literature on which he had been nourished had been created in that past. His teachers were Hellenists and more than often no more than nominal Christians. The past, and the traditions of the past, represented the finest essence of the national life as far as he was concerned, particularly the closer his world came to the inevitable collapse.

In Rome as well as in the provinces, the Gnostics, and the worshipers of Isis, of the Great Mother and of Mithra, were possibly equally as numerous as the recently ennobled, *les noveaux arrivées,* who professed to be Christians. Both Constantine the Great and his father had, in their time, been admitted to and had participated in the Gnostic mysteries, and it is worth noting that Constantine never did become a Christian until the moment he knew he was dying and it was urgent, for dynastic reasons, to "die in the faith."

These older faiths, it must be remembered, had their rules and their periods of fasting and abstinence, and a priesthood set apart from the world to a degree that the Christians could seldom equal. Isis, Mithra, Hecate, and Magna Mater could be worshipped, the worshipper explaining that, under the many names of the Pantheon, it was the attributes of the one Great Power, the Infinite One, which was truly adored. Five centuries before Christ, speculative thinkers in Greece had talked of a unity between the phantasmagoria of sense, and in the fifth century after Christ, the Neo-Platonist Macrobius could, in contrast to the constantly quarreling Christian sectaries, hold fast to this doctrine of the Infinite One from whom, through a chain of successive emanations, the Universe proceeded.

The world of the Roman was thus rich and colorful and complex, whatever faith he might nominally belong to, whatever gods he might actually pray to in the privacy of his home. It was a world for sceptics and for rebels, for disputationists and for men of faith, for ascetics and for monks such as those whom Saint Jerome (340–420 A.D.) thundered against in his letter to Eustochium:

> "There are some who wriggle their way into the priesthood of the diaconate in order to have easier access to the women. Their only concern is their clothes and their perfumes. The important thing is that their feet shouldn't float about in a pair of shoes too big for them. Their hair has a permanent wave, their fingers glitter with rings, and for fear the damp street might wet their soles, they walk on tip-toe. To look at, you would think they were fiancés, not clerics." *

Does this sound familiar? Do you by chance think of Rome in the days of the Borgias, or of France in the days of, say, Cardinal Mazarin?

* Steinmann, p. 129.

Never mind. Less than a hundred years later, Luxorius, a grammarian, a Vir Clarissimus and Spectabilis of Carthage, and incidentally a Christian, could talk of a Deacon hurrying for his mid-afternoon tavern-snack:

> "What gullet-goal enjoins you, priest, to race?
> Are psalms less pleasant than a bacchic bowl?
> In pulpits, not in wine-bars, take your place
> And raise on high, not tankards, but the
>   soul." *

In other words, we are on curiously familiar ground, whether we talk of Rome in the Augustan age (or of Julius Caesar describing how the Celts believed that souls did not become extinct, but passed after death from one body to another), or of Roman society in the last centuries of the Western Empire.

We find a cosmopolitan and mildly cynical society, more concerned with its rights and privileges than with its responsibilities, not necessarily indifferent to the menace of the Visigoths or of the Vandals but satisfied that the deluge come after them, but not in their time, in common with the French aristocrats of the 1780's. It was not that these people were effete, or afraid, as it is too easy to say from this distance in time. They were instead tired, as a ruling class. Individual schismatics and renegades might join with the invaders, just as in Gaul where the insurrectionary movement of the dispossessed farmers and restless city-slaves and craftsmen would collaborate with the Huns, but in the main the intellectuals, whether Christian or otherwise, simply waited out the remaining years, fatalists all, resigned to the inevitable.

It is against this background, first of intellectuals flourishing in a world which could never die, and then in a world which the thoughtful realized was sick within itself, and then in a world which everyone knew would soon end, perhaps in their lifetime, that we have to consider the Roman under-

* Lindsay, p. 221.

standing and at times acceptance of the concept of pre-existence from the time when Ennius (239–169 B.C.), the Calabrian poet, had written how Homer had appeared to him in a dream and had told him that their bodies had once been animated by the same soul.

Cicero (106–43 B.C.) had written how the mistakes and the sufferings of human life had made him think sometimes that the ancients had been right when they said that men were born in order to suffer the penalty for some sins committed in a former life.

He had written in *On Old Age* that the soul was of heavenly origin, forced down from its home in the highest and buried in earth, a place opposed to its divine nature and its immortality. He cited Pythagoras and the Pythagoreans who "never doubted that we had souls drafted from the Universal Divine intelligence", and the discourse of Socrates, the last day of his life, on the immortality of the soul.

"I need say no more. I have convinced myself, and I hold—in view of the rapid movement of the soul, its vivid memory of the past and its prophetic knowledge of the future, its many accomplishments, its vast range of knowledge, its numerous discoveries—that a nature embracing such varied gifts cannot itself be mortal. And since the soul is always in motion and yet has no external source of motion, for it is self-moved, I conclude that it will also have no end to its motion, because it is not likely ever to abandon itself . . .

"It is again a strong proof of men knowing most things before birth, that when mere children they grasp innumerable facts with such speed as to show that they are not then taking them in for the first time, but remembering and recalling them."

Virgil (70–19 B.C.), who told in *The Aeneid* how souls become forgetful of the former earthlife and revisit the vaulted realms of the world, willing to return again into living bodies, describes, elsewhere in *The Aeneid,* the death by suicide of Dido of Carthage: *

> "Then Juno, pitying her long agony,
> And slow release from life, sent Iris down,
> To unfetter from the limbs the struggling soul.
> For since she met with no predestined death,
> Nor merited her end, but died cut off
> Pitifully, impassioned by swift frenzy,
> Not yet had Proserpine shorn from her head
> The golden lock, and marked her for the shades.
> Then Iris, dewdrops on her golden wings,
> Trailing a thousand hues athwart the sun,
> Glided to earth and stood above her head,
> 'This sacred lock,' she cried, 'I bear to Dis,
> For so I am commanded. Thus I free you
> From mortal flesh.' With that she cut the lock,
> And as she cut the body's warmth was sped
> And life departed to the winds of heaven."

Ovid (43 B.C.–A.D. 17) had written that souls were not subject to death and that having left their former abode, "they ever inhabit new dwellings and, there received, live on."

During the succeeding centuries, Rome, preoccupied with Empire, is predictably less concerned with the human soul. There are scattered references to the subject in the writings of Lucan (A.D. 39–65), the nephew of Seneca the Younger, and in the writings of Apuleius, born circa A.D. 123, a wealthy and educated African who lived in Carthage and who is perhaps best known for his novel, "The Golden Ass". (His surviving works also include a speech delivered in his own defense after he had been charged with winning his attractive and wealthy wife by black magic. He was acquitted.)

The satirist Lucian, who lived in the second century, born at Samosata on the Euphrates, settled at Athens when he was about forty, and devoted himself to writing for many years, referred to the subject in his *The Sale of Creeds.*

* Todd, p. 99.

The Neo-Platonist Emperor Julian (A.D. 331–363), who believed himself to be a reincarnation of Alexander the Great, is quoted as saying as he lay dying on the battlefield: "I have learned from philosophy how much more excellent the soul is than the body, and that the separation of the nobler substance should be the subject of joy rather than affliction." After which he turned to his friends and, very much as had Socrates, entered into a metaphysical discussion as to the nature of the soul. (Sallustius, Pretorian Prefect under the Emperor Julian, had written: "It is not unlikely that the rejection of God is a kind of punishment: we may well believe that those who knew the gods and neglected them in one life may in another be deprived of the knowledge of them altogether.")

The end was drawing near. Roman society, throughout the last century of the Western Empire, would be preoccupied with the minutiae of life and with clinging to a formalized "understanding" of the past. While the Vandals were besieging Carthage, plays were being performed in the amphitheater. While their world fell about them in Gaul, a poet mourned:

"In village, villa, cross-roads, district, field,
    down every roadway, and at every turning,
death, grief, destruction, arson was revealed.
    In one great conflagration Gaul is burning.
Why tell the deathroll of a falling world
    which goes the accustomed way of endless fear?
Why count how many unto death are hurled
    when you may see your own day hurrying near?" *

Perhaps at the same time the poet had drawn a modicum of comfort from the fifth century commentary of the Neo-Platonist Macrobius on Cicero's *Dream of Scipio*:

"The soul is drawn down to these terrene bodies,
    and is on this account said to die when it is en-

---

* Lindsay, p. 201.

closed in this fallen region, and the seat of mortality. Nor ought it to cause any disturbance that we have so often mentioned the death of the soul, which we have pronounced to be immortal. For the soul is not extinguished by its own proper death, but is only overwhelmed for a time. Nor does it lose the benefit of perpetuity by its temporal demersion. Since, when it deserves to be purified from the contagion of vice, through its entire refinement from body, it will be restored to the light of perennial life, and will return to its pristine integrity and perfection." *

It is when we turn to the Middle Ages and to the Renaissance that the sceptic is due for a shock.

Somehow it seems right that Pythagoras and Plato and Aristotle, not to mention Cicero and Virgil, accepted the concept of pre-existence.

But we then turn, much too briefly, to consider the rediscovery of Pythagoras and Plato and Aristotle by Medieval Europe, in part through the influence of Byzantine scholars but more so because of the influence of the universities of Muslim Spain on intellectual life in these times.

Make no mistake about this. We can talk of the intellectual diversity of the thirteenth century, commonly seen as the century of St. Thomas, and in so doing talk of the Latin Averroists, Robert Grosseteste and Roger Bacon, the masters at Oxford, and of the school in Paris, in the preceding century dominated by Peter Abelard, which was striking out into new areas of speculative thought.

Oxford, in the thirteenth century, continued the twelfth-century tradition of Chartres in its quest for an encyclopedic culture and in its attachment to academic disciplines rediscovered through contact with the Arabs. An example is the translation, about 1200, of the optics or *Perspective* of Alha-

---

* See Samuel Dill, *Roman Society in the Last Century of the Western Empire*, pps. 106–112, for a more detailed discussion of Macrobius' Commentary.

zen (965–1039), the mathematician, whose theory of light represented an extrapolation from Aristotelian thought.

Roger Bacon, his pupil, tells us how Robert Grosseteste could understand both the Fathers and the philosophers. He completed and revised earlier translations from the Greek, and wrote a commentary on Aristotle's *Posterior Analytics* that was to be influential for a long time. Grosseteste's Franciscan pupil, Roger Bacon, an Aristotelian influenced by Avicenna, mathematician and philosopher, is unquestionably one of the most interesting and complex personalities in this period.

There was, in other words, a degree of intellectual ferment and vitality in this time which, bluntly, is in marked contrast to the stylistic perfection and undoubtedly greater refinement which we do find in the Renaissance.

These men, generally clerics (though it is worth noting that Roger Bacon did not enter the Franciscan Order until he was forty-three, ten years after his return to Oxford from Paris, to which he later returned), were remarkably unflappable people in this world in transition, the sophistication of which we are only now realizing.

An example is the fact that Dante and the group of poets known as the *Fideli d'Amore* used a secret language, highly symbolic, obviously with one eye on the church which already had an uncomfortable habit of descending upon the unwary who, intoxicated by the flowers of knowledge, forgot that any number of things, particularly ideas, could be considered subversive by the Establishment of the day.

With this in mind Dante and his friends had to be particularly careful, for innumerable ideas in the *Divine Comedy* were inspired by the work of the Spanish-born Sufi philosopher and poet, Ibn al 'Arabi (1164–1240). Dante had, in fact, taken the entire geography of heaven and hell from the works of Ibn al 'Arabi and other Muslim writers.

There is at least one glancing reference to the soul's return to earth when, in Canto XX *(Paradiso)*, Dante writes of meeting a Roman Emperor in the Heaven of Jupiter and being told how he had come back into his bones, the "reward of living hope."

> "The glorious soul returning to flesh where it abode awhile, believed in Him who had power to help, and believing, kindled into such a flame of Love that at the second death it was worthy to come into this joy."

The Renaissance saw an all too brief Neo-Platonist revival, climaxing decades of philosophic controversy, which had begun when Giorgio Gemistus Pletho (1335–1450), the extraordinary Byzantine philosopher, attended the Council of Florence in 1439 as a deputy of the Greek church. It was Pletho who had written:

> "As to ourselves, our soul, partaking of the divine nature, remains immortal and eternal in the precincts which are the limit of our world. Attached to a mortal envelope, it is sent by the gods now into one body, now into another, in view of the universal harmony, in order that the union of the mortal and immortal elements in human nature may contribute to the unity of the Whole."

Pletho inspired Cosimo de Medici with the idea of founding an academy of Platonists in Florence and, with this in mind, Marsilio Ficino, the son of Cosimo's chief physician, began his studies in Greek language and philosophy. He completed his first work on the Platonic Institutions when only twenty-three. By the time he was thirty he was beginning his translation of Plato, later translating Plotinus and Iamblichos. It is worth noting that he also wrote a treatise on the Platonic doctrine of immortality.

When Lorenzo, Cosimo's grandson, was eight, Ficino became his tutor, and when Lorenzo de Medici became the head of the house he not only brought his grandfather's plans to completion but also founded a university in Pisa, established public libraries for the people of Florence, and became the patron of Michelangelo, Botticelli, and Leonardo da Vinci. Lorenzo and Ficino, aided by Giovanni Pico, son of the Prince of Mirandola, who is described as deeply versed in the learning of the Chaldeans, Hebrews and Arabians, contributed considerably to the revival of Neo-Platonism. With the death of these three the Academy they had started went out of existence. It had by that time made a major contribution to the advancement of art, science, and philosophy, and to the spread of Platonism, in the Europe of their time.

Giordano Bruno (1548–1600), who was burnt at the stake, had held that souls were immortal and that they might pass from body to body. His contemporary, Sir Francis Bacon (1561–1626), possibly towards the end of his rather eventful life, had written wryly in a letter:

"And since I have lost much time with this age,
I would be glad, as God shall give me leave,
To recover it with posterity."

In the following century, Cambridge University in England became the center of a movement that attracted considerable attention in its day. Its leaders were known as the Cambridge Platonists, the most prominent among them being Henry More, whom Samuel Johnson was to call "one of our greatest divines and philosophers and no mean poet," and Ralph Cudworth whose encyclopedic *The True Intellectual System of the Universe,* published in London in 1678, was subtitled, "A storehouse of learning on the ancient opinions of the nature, origin, pre-existence, transmigration, and future of the soul." Cudworth agreed with the Greek view that in order for the soul to be immortal after death, it must have existed prior to birth. George Berkeley, the Irish bishop and philosopher, became a professed adherent of what could be described as the Cudworth school.

We find David Hume (1711–1776) in his *The Immortality of the Soul,* Thomas Taylor (1758–1835), in his introduction to his translation of the works of Plato and Thomas Carlyle

(1795–1881), in *Sartor Resartus,* among those who obviously, at least in principle, accepted the concept.

It is with the twentieth century however that we receive the promised shock because these men and these women who accept the concept, calmly and objectively, are in no sense of the word considered to be mystics and metaphysically oriented. These are in the main products of our society and our times, men of some prominence in the world we know, in arts and letters and in the sciences.

Queen Victoria's favorite author, Marie Corelli (1885–1924), Sir Rider Haggard (1885–1925), Sir Arthur Conan Doyle (1859–1930), and Talbot Mundy (1879–1940) are perhaps explainable in view of special individual interests (in the case of Doyle in Spiritualism). But it is worth noting that Rudyard Kipling (1865–1936), particularly in his short story, "The Finest Story in the World"; Arnold Bennett (1867–1931); John Buchan (1875–1940), author and Governor General of Canada; and the late Somerset Maugham, likewise accepted the concept. Maugham pointed out in his autobiography that it would be less difficult to bear the evils of one's own life if one understood that they resulted from one's errors in a previous existence.

When we consider the interest in this subject in Germany we may have reason to be startled if we subscribe to the usual generalizations about the German mind.

To do so is of course as unwise as to cite the former Governor of Alabama and the late Senator Robert Kennedy and, let us say, the late Reverend Martin Luther King, as examples of the *genus Americanus.* In a sense it would be correct to do so; in a larger sense it would be incorrect and, similarly, no facile generalization is possible when discussing the extraordinarily schizoid and almost Japanese modern German mind, in all its regional manifestations.

It is a mind capable of reaching extraordinary heights in the arts and letters, particularly in music, and it is a mind capable of plumbing unfathomable depths, witness Hitler, witness Goering, witness Goebbels, witness Haushofer, witness Eichmann. And in the same breath you must of course add the names of those who, from the beginning or later, for somewhat less than self-less reasons, fought against all that these men stood for. Valiantly, if belatedly.

The German character, as destiny-ridden as the Japanese, cannot be blamed solely on the Prussians, or on the reaction to the defeat after the First World War. The German mind, for we are considering an all-German mind, whatever its politics, whatever its provincial accent, was forged in the days of the Imperial French occupation of Germany more than a hundred years earlier by those anti-occupation intellectuals who even then foresaw Germany's later historic role in a changed Europe.

The Germans have always responded to the Old Gods. They did so in Caesar's time. They did it, symbolically, in Luther's time, when the one-time monk called for a revolt against foreign-based ecclesiastical overlordship. And they did it in the days prior to the French Revolution, and in the years that followed, when the secret societies, representing intellectuals as well as office-holders, banded together against the Establishment of the day, invoking the Mysteries in their search for, professedly, democracy.

The role of the metaphysically oriented secret societies at this stage of German history cannot be over-estimated. They had contacts everywhere, adherents everywhere, who made the societies' claim to omniscience a tangible reality. The curious thing is of course that men gave their lives in those days for causes that differed only in the historical perspective of the actors. They all died—or worked for—what they understood to be Germany's destiny, very much as the Communists and the National Socialists and, for that matter, the Social Democrats in the days before the Third Reich, each in reality likewise shared the same dream. (I might add that I have little patience with those who think the Kremlin's realpolitik is something new. No Swede, no Finn, no Balt, has forgotten Czar Peter.)

It is worth noting that among the ranks of those who accepted the probability of Reincarnation is that rather complex man, Frederick the Great (1712–1786) who, shortly before his death, felt certain that the more noble part of him would not cease to live upon his death. Though he might not be a king in his future life, this was not important, so long as he lived an active life and, on top of this, earned less ingratitude.

Immanuel Kant's *Critique of Pure Reason,* published in 1781, had opened a new period in metaphysical thought, at least in Germany. What Kant proposed, when he undertook to transfer attention from the objects that engaged the mind to the mind itself, has been called a revolution in metaphysics comparable to the Copernican revolution in astronomy. Goethe, Schiller, Hegel and Schopenhauer are among the Kantians whose contribution to this school of thought can be cited. The transcendental movements in England and America were much influenced by these German thinkers; vide Carlyle's championship of the cause of German philosophy and literature in the English reviews, Coleridge's visit to Germany in the company of Wordsworth, and Raiph Waldo Emerson's publication of Carlyle's articles in the United States.

Kant had talked of "the endless duration of the immortal soul throughout the infinity of time", and G. E. Lessing (1729–1781) had wondered aloud whether the hypothesis of Metempsychosis was ridiculous merely because it was the oldest, because the human intellect had adopted it without demur "before men's minds had been distracted and weakened by the sophistry of the schools." Elsewhere he had asked why it was so certain that his soul had only once "inhabited the form of man? Is it after all so unreasonable to suppose that my soul, upon its journey to perfection, should have been forced to wear this fleshly veil more than once?"

J. G. von Herder (1744–1803) had talked about those men whom we all know—you immediately think of Manly Palmer Hall, for one—who cannot possibly have become what they were in one single human existence. And J. W. von Goethe (1749–1832) had written that he was certain that he had been here as he was then a thousand times before and he hoped to return a thousand times. He could not explain to a mutual friend, or so he put it, his relations with Charlotte von Stein or her influence over him, except by the theory of Metempsychosis. As he had said in a poem to her, he was certain that they had been kin, or married, in former lives.

The list is close to endless. Johann Heinrich Zschokke (1771–1848) wrote how he hoped one day, in another world, in another life, to be united again with those whom he had loved in that life. Heinrich von Kleist (1777-1811), the dramatist and poet; Gotthilf Heinrich von Schubert (1780–1860), naturalist and philosopher; Friedrich Ruckert (1788–1866), the poet and orientalist; and even Heinrich Heine (1797–1856), each accepted the concept, at least intellectually. Heine wondered, whimsically, if the soul of Pythagoras occupied the unfortunate student who failed his exams because of his inability to prove the Pythagorean theory.

Arthur Schopenhauer (1788–1860) wrote how the personality disappeared at death, but that nothing was lost thereby because this personality was a being ignorant of time and therefore knowing neither life nor death. When we died we threw off this personality like a worn-out garment (it seems clear he was thinking here of the physical personality and not the psychic), and rejoiced because we were about to receive a new and better one. He called Europe that part of the world which was haunted by the incredible delusion that man was created out of nothing and that his present birth was his first entrance into life.

It is when we come to Richard Wagner (1813–1883), who more than most molded what we know, or think we know, as the German character, that we find the earlier mentioned schizoid qualities most clearly visible, beginning with the warning of the dying Rienzi, in Wagner's first opera, written and composed when he was twenty-five, that:

". . . as long as the eternal city will not pass away, you shall see Rienzi return again."

In a letter to a friend, written in 1860, he wrote that only

Reincarnation could give him any consolation, since that belief showed how all could at least reach complete redemption. He saw "the spotless purity of Lohengrin" (Wagner's phrase) explained in the fact that he was the continuation of Parsifal, who had had to fight for his purity. And in an earlier letter he flatly called the doctrine of the transmigration of souls the basis of a truly human life.

This from the man whose name, after his death, was to have quite other connotations.

Friedrich Nietzche (1844–1900) is another German who unexpectedly, if we keep in mind what he in his turn has been credited with by *his* interpreters, once wrote that his doctrine was to live so that he might desire to live again—it was one's duty for, in any case, one would live again!

Rainer Maria Rilke (1875–1926) is quoted as considering Russia his soul-home, convinced that he had lived in Moscow in a former incarnation. Franz Werfel (1890–1945) suggested in his novel, *Star of the Unborn*, that a hundred thousand years from now a man who had passed through many rebirths would have the privilege of learning what happened in the millenia following his death.

Assuming, Werfel might have added, he knew how to obtain the knowledge.

With rare exceptions the men referred to above, at the same time as they accepted the concept of Reincarnation as Richard Wagner obviously did, perhaps predictably so assumed that the laws of this concept did not apply to them. As a result, during the days of the Third Reich, we saw the development within Germany of a rather strange school of thought which I suppose may be described as Wagnerian metaphysics, designed for a master race which, blessed by the Old Gods, was to rule forever.

Let us now consider those among us who, in addition to the American transcendentalists, likewise accepted this concept of pre-existence.

There is of course that doughty non-conformist, B. Franklin, printer, who expressed the certainty, in his Epitaph, that "the Work" was to appear once more in a new and more elegant edition, obviously "revised and corrected by the Author". He would not object, he wrote elsewhere, to this "new edition", he only hoped that the *errata* of the last might by then be corrected.

We have already touched on the marked influence of the German transcendentalists upon the American movement. *Vide* Emerson's essay on Plato (the Platonic philosophers were studied, incidentally, in the original Greek), and his description of Wordsworth's "The Ode to Immortality," as the best modern essay on the subject.

An important contribution to American Transcendentalism came from the Orient. Copies of the first English translations of the Bhagavad-Gita, the Upanishads, the Vedas and the Puranas were obtained by Emerson, Thoreau and others, Thoreau translating from the French and publishing a Sanskrit story, "The Transmigration of Seven Brahmins."

It was Ralph Waldo Emerson who called the soul "an emanation of the Divinity, a part of the soul of the world," which came from the outside of the human body, "as into a temporary abode", after which it went out of it again.

Paraphrasing the Upanishad, Emerson wrote that the soul was not born and that it did not die. "Unborn, eternal, it is not slain, though the body is slain."

Henry David Thoreau called the idea of transmigration unavoidable, "not merely a fancy of the poets, but an instinct of the race." On another occasion he wrote, revealing his own deep faith in the concept:

"I lived in Judea eighteen hundred years ago, but I never knew that there was such a one as Christ among my contemporaries.

"And Hawthorne, too, I remember as one with whom I sauntered in old heroic times along the banks of the Scamander amid the ruins of chariots and heroes . . . As the stars looked to me when I was a shepherd in Assyria, they look to me now a New Englander . . . As far back as I can remember, I have unconsciously referred to the experiences of a previous state of existence."

On the other hand, Lafcadio Hearn (1850-1904), who lived in the United States for over twenty years, experienced only pain as he "saw" his former births. He welcomed the return to the present only to be told by "the divine one" (possibly a hypnotist?) who had brought him back that others had likewise "been permitted to see something of their pre-existence. But no one of them ever could endure to look far. Power to see all former births belongs to those externally released from the bonds of self. Such exist outside of illusion, —outside of form and name; and pain cannot come nigh them. But to you, remaining in illusion, not even the Buddha would give power to look back more than a little way."

C. J. Ducasse, former Chairman of the Department of Philosophy, Brown University, and Past President, American Philosophical Association, was quoted in the Providence *Evening Bulletin* for June 26, 1958, as saying: "The concept of rebirth on earth, perhaps after an interval occupied by the individual in distilling out of memories of a life just ended such wisdom as his reflective powers enabled him to extract, would enable him to believe there is justice in the universe."

It is an incredible list of the all-time greats in American letters and philosophy who obviously, quietly and without fanfare, suscribe to the concept of Reincarnation. Henry Wadsworth Longfellow, John Greenleaf Whittier ("We shape ourselves the joy or fear of which the coming life is made . . ."), Walt Whitman ("I know I am deathless . . ."), James Russell Lowell, Thomas Bailey Aldrich, Joaquin Miller, Vachel Lindsay, Kahlil Gibran ("Yes, I shall return with the time, and though death may hide me and the greater silence enfold me, yet again will I seek your understanding . . ."), Mark Twain, David Belasco, Jack London, and, in a sense, William Faulkner, all shared this belief.

As did that extraordinary American, General Homer Lea, the friend of Dr. Sun Yat Sen, who, like Napoleon, considered himself a "man of destiny", and who, also like Napoleon, speculating upon his own peculiarities, felt these were derived from other lives. Lea was an extraordinary military strategist whom even the German Emperor Wilhelm respected.

There is no doubt a temptation, at this point, to pause and to wonder, perhaps plaintively, *why* this procession of names and quotes from men who've in the main gone to their reward, recently or in times past, whatever this reward may have been.

You mutter to yourself that you believe in Reincarnation. That you don't need all this. *You* know that *you* know thus and thus, and that is enough!

But, of course, that isn't so.

Apart from the reality that if you do accept the concept you need still to understand that you are not only not alone but part of a tradition that is fully as old as written history, you must know, as a student, that there is no one time in your days or in your years that can be set aside for learning. You begin to know the new world around you while you are still in your cradle. You learn gradually to use the tools which are necessary for survival in this new world. And, so long as you are a part of this new world, you continue to learn, to study, to seek out the truth—not from those who tell you that they have the answers to the world's ills, spiritual and otherwise—but instead from those who seek to help you to understand the Inner You, and to strengthen that Inner You, and to free it from hate and fear and envy and all the other sicknesses which are a part of the Outer You.

Yes. This section is for those who accept the concept of Reincarnation, and equally so for those who need to understand that this is not something mouthed at you by some men in saffron robes, something alien, seomething strange, but instead a part of the memory of the race, something which has been known to Man for thousands of years, in many countries and to many men.

Many of the people who have accepted the concept have shown by their actions that they did not understand what they professed to believe. This has been particularly true throughout the past two hundred years when you could find a

Voltaire or a Wagner obviously accepting the concept without recognizing that the laws of this concept applied to him also.

This is particularly true also in the case of many of those scientists who have accepted, intellectually, the concept of pre-existence or Reincarnation. Dr. Henry More mentioned Girolamo Cardan (1501-1576), the noted Italian physician, mathematician, and philosopher, and Johannes Fernelius (Jean Fernel, 1497-1558), the French doctor and writer whom many called "the modern Galen".

To these we must add Paracelsus (1493-1541), the first man to write scientific books in language that the common man could understand and who, as some of you no doubt know, has been credited with the discovery of Mesmerism. Philippus Aureolus Theophrastus Bombastus von Hohenheim, known as Paracelsus, was a Neo-Platonist. He wrote on one occasion: "Life is something spiritual. Life is not only in that which moves, such as men and animals, but in all things; for what would be a corporeal form without a spirit? The form may be destroyed; but the spirit remains and is living, for it is the subjective life. . . ." The body which we receive from our parents, he continued, "has no spiritual powers, for wisdom and virtue, faith, hope and charity, do not grow from the earth. These powers are not the products of man's physical organization, but the attributes of another invisible and glorified body, whose germs are laid within man."

Several hundred years later Camille Flammarion (1842-1925), the astronomer, wondered whether we were at long last returning to doctrines first taught seven thousand years earlier. "Yes, and no. Yes, in the sense that the ancients knew more about these things than is generally supposed. No, in the sense that present scientific methods have brought practical confirmation and the beginning of an explanation."

Thomas Edison (1847-1931), one of the early members of the Theosophical Society, was asked by reporters during his last illness if he believed in survival after death. His answer was that the only survival he could conceive of was to start a new earth cycle again.

Sir Oliver Lodge (1851-1940), the physicist, and James Ward (1843-1925), Professor of Mental Philosophy at Cambridge from 1897 to 1925, are among the many others who frankly accepted the concept. And Carl G. Jung (1875-1961), the psychiatrist and psychologist, is quoted as writing that "Rebirth is an affirmation that must be counted among the primordial affirmations of mankind."

Dr. Ian Stevenson, Chairman, Department of Psychiatry, University of Virginia School of Medicine, warned, in an article some years ago, against arbitrary conclusions, either pro or con. While he felt that Reincarnation was the most plausible "hypothesis" for understanding the cases he had cited in his "The Evidence for Survival from Claimed Memories of Former Incarnations", he warned that the cases, considered by themselves, did not prove Reincarnation, either singly or together. It was however clear that a large number of cases in which the recall of true memories is a plausible hypothesis should make that hypothesis worthy of attention.

The key word there is *true*.

Let us now consider, though much too briefly, the approach of Spiritualists to this concept of Reincarnation.

But first, keep in mind that when there is this talk of the case for an After Life, this represents in the main an effort to conceive of it within the framework of our limited understanding of the faith of our fathers.

The difficulty is that we are the prisoners of our own man-made myths. The reality has to be faced that the Truths, as taught by a Prophet, whether his name be Jesus or Mohammed, are at the mercy of successive interpretants as an act of joyous surrender to a God force becomes not the act of a man in momentary communion with that force but a ritualized interpretation of that communion, the minutiae of that ritual added to it by men whose skills are those of an administrator, but who would have been uncomfortable, to put it mildly, if face to face with a St. Jerome or, for that matter, with the Prophet Mohammed himself.

Those of us who consider ourselves to be Christians have a tendency not necessarily to sneer but to be uncomfortable when confronted with those whom we like to think of as primitive Christians, denominationally or otherwise. We neither understand them nor recognize that if we were to be brought back in time to attend the assemblies of those schismatic Jews who gathered together in the Catacombs or in Aleppo or in Jerusalem itself there would have been a similar absence of ritual, in our present-day understanding of the word, and only the preaching and communal sharing of the message of a man whom some said had been the Son of God, and who had lived and died in Roman Judea not too long before.

Depending on the social background of the congregants, the often "primitive" Spiritualist churches, and there are many of them throughout the world, are mostly concerned with bridging the gap between those who have survived and those who have passed on. With obvious exceptions, there is only peripheral concern in Spiritualism with this question of Reincarnation. It is blithely assumed that, out there in the ether, possibly in alternate worlds, latterday Islands of the Blessed, the dead live on, guarding us, protecting us, watching over us.

We have in other words not changed during these past two and a half thousand years, here in the West. We still hesitate to probe beyond the Veil, almost atavistically fearing the Unknown.

The result? Ecumenicism—Fellowshipping if you wish— does not flower on sterile soil.

But we digress. Let us instead talk about the French professor, Hippolyte Leon Denizard-Rivail, contemporary of Honoré de Balzac, Alexandre Dumas *fils,* Chateaubriand and Théophile Gautier, who wrote under the name of Allan Kardec. He had been told that this had been his name in a former incarnation as a Druid.

A professor teaching mathematics, astronomy, physiology, French, physics, chemistry and comparative anatomy, a disciple of Pestalozzi, Rivail was anything but a mystic. Born in

Lyons in 1804, he devoted the first part of his life to his chosen profession, publishing several works in the field of education, no more concerned with religion and spiritual matters than others in that age. It was not until he was in his early fifties that he became concerned, and at first aghast, at the widespread interest in table "rapping". Even Napoleon III, extremely interested, organized some sessions at court and was said to have carried on some lengthy conversations with whomever or whatever responded at these sessions. When asked *Who is there?*, the table would inevitably reply, via the raps, *Spirits of those you call dead*, but nobody, apparently not even the Emperor, seems to have troubled to follow up the implications of this reply. The society of the Second Empire was in any event not noted for its concern about possibly troublesome Tomorrows, or about answers to awkward questions. Tomorrow would take care of itself. It was true that some called it the age of reason and that it undeniably was an age of scepticism and materialism. Ironically, the reaction against materialism was to be started by matter itself—matter moving about, giving signs of what appeared to be life, apparently controlled by an intelligence, all in a manner at variance with known physical laws.

Rivail, beginning with noting down the messages received, through one or another method, was concerned at first only with systematising a great wealth of uncertain material. At first it had been simply table-rapping. Then variants of the same. And finally automatic writing by a medium in a trance. Rivail, writing as Kardec—he had decided to use the name when writing on the occult—collected messages received at several groups, checking the answers collected through one medium with those from another, and witnessing happenings that defied explanation. At sessions with one family where the sisters served as mediums, answers were being given on subjects about which the sisters knew nothing, including answers to questions which he had posed mentally. As far as he was concerned the mere fact of the communication with the spirits, quite apart from anything they might have to say, proved the existence of an invisible world.

The first edition of Kardec's *The Book of Spirits,* published in 1857, consisted of 1,018 questions and answers, recorded at sessions with more than ten mediums. The first part of the book dealt with what he termed primary causes, such as God, the elements of the universe and the vital principle; the second part concerned itself with the world of the spirits themselves, the incarnation of the spirit, the return of the spirit after the death of the body, Reincarnation, the plurality of inhabited worlds (in 1857!), progressive transmigration to more advanced planets, the destiny of children after death, and the spirits' return to earthly life, and why we do not remember our past incarnations. (Metempsychosis was described as beyond the bounds of possibility.) The third part, the most important in the eyes of those who were to come after him, dealt with purely moral laws, as did, in a sense, the fourth part.

Kardec, in this and his later works, *The Book of Mediums,* the fundamental mechanics of communication with the spirits, and *The Gospels As Interpreted By Spiritism*—described as presenting a full understanding of our past, present and future lives—was to influence millions of people throughout the world. Of particular interest to us at this time are some of the Divine Laws, or Laws of Nature which rule the universe, about which Kardec wrote.

> "There are innumerable inhabited worlds throughout the universe, in different stages of evolution, development and progress. The peri-spirit and physical body take on the form which is most adequate for whatever world the spirit is inhabiting."

The spirit, Kardec was told, is enveloped in a semi-material body called a peri-spirit, which personifies the spirit and give it its exterior individuality. The spirit is connected to the body itself via this peri-spirit. When the body can no longer function, then the spirit, enveloped in the peri-spirit, will leave it. This is what we call death. The act of taking or being born in a human body is known as Reincarnation; similarly the spirit with an earthly body is held to be an incarnate spirit.

The peri-spirit is composed of both electricity, the "magnetic fluid", and, to some extent, of matter.

Spirits evolve and progress through successive incarnations until perfection is attained and further incarnations are no longer necessary. Experience is acquired in each incarnation, in different ages, environments, countries and planets. What is learned in one incarnation is not forgotten in another though the physical body, the physical brain, is seldom made aware by the spirit of these experiences in previous lives. At the same time, the qualities acquired in earlier incarnations were there in the form of talents or inclinations to evil. The conscience was the voice of the spirit and would always point to the right way. As far as the world was concerned, here was a new man; in the eyes of God, Kardec said, here was a spirit with a new opportunity.

> "Spirits are the individualization of the Intelligent Principle of the Universe. They were created by God simple, ignorant and with their own free will. Exercising this free will, they progress through multiple incarnations and evolve to ever higher stages of intelligence and love."

Before each incarnation, the spirit would be connected to the body, while still in the mother's womb, through the peri-spirit. Upon birth, or rebirth, the spirits' faculties would re-awaken in the body at the same time as the organs' ability to express the spirit's qualities developed and grew.

> "To progress along the path of spiritual evolution, there are two main requirements. The first is to love one another. The second is to acquire knowledge."

According to Kardec, science uncovered the laws governing the material world, while spiritism (or spiritualism) was the science uncovering the laws governing the spiritual world. The appearances of angels told of in the Bible were now known to have been visitations of disincarnate spirits.

God had sent superior spirits to incarnate on earth from time to time and to teach the laws of God. Each had performed his task according to the circumstances of the times and the extent to which he had drawn upon his own powers. When the spirits were asked who was the highest spirit ever to incarnate in this way and for this purpose, the answer was a terse, "Jesus."

Kardec told his readers that this was what the spirits themselves had dictated. If the reader's reason said NO, then he should simply refuse to believe what he was being told and reject the message. Millions throughout the world, including Brazil—more about that in a moment—have accepted the message. This, as far as they are concerned, describes the law which governs all spirits throughout the universe.

We are not concerned here with communications from the Beyond, or with poems or novels dictated by the dead. These are many and impressive. These include descriptions of life within the spiritual sphere the newly dead are taken to, a new approach to the Adam myth, and, in the case of a novel which claims to be the true story of St. Paul, dictated to the Brazilian medium Francisco Candido Xavier, we are told that it was not Jesus who spoke to St. Paul on the road to Damascus; it was Stephen, the first Christian martyr, whom Paul himself had helped condemn to death, who was his constant spiritual companion and guide.

In one of these books, this one authored by a spirit who claims to have been a famous doctor in his last incarnation, the spirit describes its world including the "reincarnation department" which prepares the "moulds" of the physical body of spirits who are about to incarnate again on earth. On one of his visits to this department he wonders about the significance of a dark spot he has noticed in one of the "moulds". His guide explains that this organ will be subjected to an illness at a certain stage of development of the newly incarnated spirit, the result of excesses indulged in during the spirit's last incarnation.

Many mediums, including some in Brazil where the above mentioned books were published, warn of approaching catastrophes, one describing graphically what will happen as an enormous new planet is drawn into our system. Continents will be destroyed and the poles de-iced*, with the Chosen, who are to survive the catastrophe and found the Third Millenium, seated on the right side of Christ. Divine Law operates through electromagnetic force and its wavelengths. Those whose wavelengths automatically identify them as bad will sit on the other side and will be magnetically drawn, by those same wavelengths, to the new planet about to enter our system, where evolution is in a state comparable to our Stone Age.**

Pedro McGregor, in his extremely interesting *Jesus Of The Spirits*, a study of the spiritualist movements in Brazil, quotes the head of the *Temple of Universal Religion* in Rio de Janeiro on a subject which reflects the thinking of the millions in Brazil who adhere to one or another of these groups.***

---

* One of the findings of the International Geophysical Year in 1958 was that both Poles were defrosting at a rate higher than ever before.

** Researchers who, while Spiritualists, do not accept the concept of Reincarnation, raise the possibility that some of the incidents told of in the Bridey Murphy case may either have occurred in the subject's own life or represented deeply buried memories. A classic example is that of the trance medium, Hélène Smith, who was studied by Professor Th. Flournoy over a period of several years, and who claimed at least four different incarnations, as a Hindu Princess, as Marie Antoinette, as Cagliostro, and one on the planet Mars. Drawings were made (automatically) of men, scenes and animals on Mars, and a whole language was depicted, in hieroglyphics, and "messages" were given in this Martian language. Unfortunately the whole of this material was proved to be subconscious in origin. The whole structure of the language (for further details on this see Flournoy's FROM INDIA TO THE PLANET MARS) was shown to have been modelled on the French language, the medium's native tongue. The whole Martian cycle, as well as the other cycles, were shown to be an elaborate subconscious dramatization, or at least as far as the researchers were concerned.

*** p. 236, McGregor. The Temple also contends that intelligence or intelligent life flourishes in billions of galaxies, and that this planet is one of the more inferior ones.

"Jesus is the oldest and most evolved spirit that has ever incarnated upon Earth. He was born, and died, the same way as everybody else. His spiritual nature, or his discondensed body, continues to live, as is the case with any of us. The difference is in degree of evolvement. Universal Religion says to all men: Each one of you will become a Jesus one day, each one of you will be the carrier of a torch to light a lower sphere, a planet whose stage of evolvement will be similar to ours when Jesus came. Jesus himself happens to be millions of years ahead of us. The dynamics of the universe have it that those with more light guide those with less, so Jesus is truly our Lord, our Sun of love and wisdom. He reached this stage by evolution; and one day we shall reach it too."

V

CAN YOU BE A CHRISTIAN AND STILL BELIEVE IN REINCARNATION?

Can you be a Christian and still believe in Reincarnation? Yes!

If you believe in Reincarnation you see Man as an immortal spiritual self, born into physical bodies many times throughout his long evolutionary journey to perfection.

There is in reality no conflict there with the original teachings of the Church!

What we must keep in mind at this point is that the Gospels we know are not the Gospels the Fathers of the Church knew and taught and were ready to defend with their lives. Our "orthodox" versions of the Old and the New Testaments, ignoring for the moment the errors and omissions (not to mention the sins and omissions) of still later "authorities", date back no further than to the sixth century, to the Fifth Ecumenical Congress of Constantinople. The exclusion from the Christian creed of the teaching of the pre-existence of the soul and, by implication, of Reincarnation, dates back to this Congress. Succeeding centuries have close to sanctified as irrefutable dogma these purely political decisions of Justinian and the Congress. When therefore a popular writer in this field can talk of how his "entire intellectual, emotional, and religious bias is against reincarnation", this is understandable because our times do not demand a knowledge of our past; it is difficult enough to know the present.

There is however no conflict on this subject. The Fathers of the Church, before Justinian and even before Constantine, accepted and believed in Reincarnation. Indeed the Apostles themselves referred repeatedly to the concept of pre-existence as when St. Paul quoted God as saying to Rebecca, about the still-to-be-born children, "Jacob have I loved, but Esau have I hated." (Romans 9:13), and St. John stated, in Revelations 3:12, "Him that overcometh will I make a pillar in the temple of my God and he shall go no more out." Here is the ages-old concept, common at the time to Hellenicised Judaism as well as to the members of the new movement within Judaism, of the ordained exile of the soul and the need for it to be purified by long wandering before it could be admitted as a "pillar in the temple of God."

Philo Judaeus (20 B.C.–A.D. 54) had written, "The Air is full of souls; those who are nearest to earth descending to be tied to mortal bodies, desiring to live in them." Elsewhere he elaborated on this:

> "The company of disembodied souls is distributed in various orders. The law of some of them is to enter mortal bodies and after certain prescribed periods be again set free. But those possessed of a diviner structure are absolved from all local bonds of earth. Some of these souls choose confinement in mortal bodies because they are earthly and corporeally inclined . . ."

Flavius Josephus (A.D. 37–100), addressing some Jewish soldiers who had been ready to kill themselves rather than be captured by the Romans, had protested:

> "The bodies of all men are, indeed, mortal, and are created out of corruptible material; but the soul is ever immortal, and is a portion of the divinity that inhabits our bodies. . . . Do ye not remember that all pure Spirits when they depart out of this life obtain a most holy place in heaven, from whence, in the revolutions of ages, they are again sent into pure bodies; while the souls of those of those who have committed self-destruction are doomed to a region in the darkness of Hades?"

That Jesus and his contemporaries accepted this concept, without either thinking about it or arguing about it, is clear from the time when there was brought before Jesus a man who had been born blind. The disciples wondered why he had been thus punished and asked Jesus, "Which did sin, this man or his parents?" (John 9:34). As far as they were concerned it was obvious that if this man had been born blind, his sin, assuming there had been a sin, could not have been committed in *this* life.

And there is of course the famous passage in Matthew (17:9-13):

> "And as they came down from the mountain, Jesus charged them, saying, Tell the vision to no man, until the Son of man be risen again from the dead.
>
> "And the disciples asked him, saying, Why then say the scribes that Elias must first come? And Jesus answered and said unto them, Elias truly shall first come, and restore all things. But I say unto you, that Elias is come already, and they knew him not, but have done unto him whatsoever they listed. Likewise shall also the Son of man suffer of them.
>
> "Then the disciples understood that he spoke unto them of John the Baptist."

While Justin Martyr (A.D. 100–165) expressly spoke of the soul inhabiting more than once the human body, but denied that on taking "a second time" this embodied form it could remember previous experiences, this anti-Pythagorean approach was challenged by others among the Early Church Fathers. St. Clement of Alexandria (A.D. 150–220), who is described by Arnobius, towards the end of the third century, as having written several wonderful stories about metempsychosis "and many worlds before Adam," wrote in his "Exhortation to the Pagans":

> "We were in being long before the foundation of the world; we existed in the eye of God, for it is our destiny to live in Him. We are the reasonable

creatures of the Divine Word; therefore, we have existed from the beginning, for in the beginning was the Word. . . . Not for the first time does He show pity on us in our wanderings, He pitied us from the very beginning. . . . Philolaus, the Pythagorean, taught that the soul was flung into the body as a punishment for the misdeeds it had committed, and his opinion was confirmed by the most ancient of the prophets."

In *Divinorum Institutionem* Lactantius, tutor of the son of Constantine the Great, whom St. Jerome (for a variety of less than saintly reasons) called the Christian Cicero, stated bluntly that the soul was capable of immortality and of bodily survival only on the hypothesis that it existed before the body.

His contemporary, St. Gregory, Bishop of Nyssa (A.D. 257–332), had written that it was absolutely necessary that the soul be healed and purified. "If this does not take place during its life on earth it must be accomplished in future lives."

St. Augustine (354–430) asks in his *Confessions:*

"Say, Lord to me . . . say, did my infancy succeed another age of mine that died before it? Was it that which I spent within my mother's womb? . . . and what before that life again, O God my joy, was I anywhere or in any body? For this I have none to tell me, neither father nor mother, nor experience of others, nor mine own memory."

In *Contra Academicos*, St. Augustine comments in passing: "The message of Plato, the purest and most luminous in all philosophy, has at least scattered the darkness of error, and now shines forth mainly in Plotinus, a Platonist so like his master that one would think they lived together, or rather —since so long a period of time separates them—that Plato is born again in Plotinus."

We have thus the witness, both of the Apostles and of St. Augustine, St. Gregory, St. Clement of Alexandria, and of countless others, to the widespread acceptance by the early church fathers of the doctrine of the pre-existence of the soul. This was largely due to the influence of the teachings of Origen* (A.D. 185–254) whom St. Jerome at one time designated "the greatest teacher of the Church after the apostles." Origen had been concerned with correlating the established Christian teachings of the day (it must be remembered this was long before the attempt to reconcile the warring factions at the Council of Nicea) with the quasi-Christian dogmas of Plato, Aristotle, Numenius and Corrutus. (Stranger things than this were to happen to his teachings in succeeding centuries.) Christ was to Origen as the Logos who is the Father from eternity, to whom alone the instructed Christian directed his thoughts, requiring nothing more than a divine teacher. Origen explained the actual sinfulness of all men by the theological hypothesis of the pre-existence and the premundane fall of each soul.

In his *De Principiis* he had written:

> "Every soul . . . comes into this world strengthened by the victories or weakened by the defeats of its previous life. Its place in this world as a vessel appointed to honor or dishonor is determined by its previous merits or demerits. Its work in this world determines its place in the world which is to follow this."

In his *Contra Celsum* he has also written:

> "Is it not more in conformity with reason that every soul, for certain mysterious reasons (I speak now according to the opinions of Pythagoras ** and

* Origenes Adamantius.

** Pythagoras asserted that he had received the memory of all his soul's transmigrations as a gift from Mercury, along with the gift of recollecting what his own soul, and the souls of others, had experienced between death and rebirth.

Plato, and Empedocles, whom Celcus frequently names), is introduced into a body according to its deserts and former actions? Is it not rational that souls who have used their bodies to do the utmost possible good should have a right to bodies endowed with qualities superior to the bodies of others?

"The soul, which is immaterial and invisible in its nature, exists in no material place without having a body suited to the nature of that place; accordingly, it at one time puts off one body, which was necessary before, but which is no longer adequate in its changed status, and it exchanges it for a second."

Origen's teachings were regarded as based solidly on what at that time had been accepted as the true gospels. Even St. Jerome, who at times differed with Origen (as indeed he did with most), agreed with Origen's interpretation of, "Who hath chosen us before the foundation of the world?" (St. Paul's *Ephesians* 1:4) and stated:

"A divine habitation, and a true rest above, I think, is to be understood, where rational creatures dwelt, and where, before their descent to a lower position, and removal from the invisible to the visible, and fall to earth, and need of gross bodies, they enjoyed a former blessedness. Whence God the Creator made for them bodies suitable to their humble position, and created this visible world and sent into the world ministers for their salvation."

The Anathemas pronounced by this Fifth Council or Synod against what was described as Origenism represented a politically inspired and nearly successful attempt to expunge from the pages of history, *de facto* and canonically, teachings which were widely accepted in the West. It was a victory for the Monophysite dogma to which the Emperor Justinian and, more important, the Empress Theodora, had become converted. The Monophysites contended that Jesus' physical body was wholly divine, and had never at any time combined divine and human attributes. This represented a total rejection of the teachings of Origen who not only believed in predestination, but also taught that Christ the Logos, or Word, inhabited the human body of Jesus, thus sanctifying it. The Monophysites had continued to provoke strife and discord until A.D. 451 when a specially summoned Church Council, overwhelmingly loyal as was most of the West to Origen's teachings, had in a sense split Christ into two separate natures, human and divine. One of Justinian's first public acts—this before he came under the influence of Theodora—had been to make the Patriarch of Constantinople declare his full adhesion to the decisions of this Council, known as the Chalcedonian Decree. But, within a matter of years, he was to permit a local synod of bishops to formally discredit and condemn the writings of Origen and, ten years later, came the much-debated conclusions of the Fifth Council, formally convoked to deal not with Origenism but with other matters.

It must be remembered that not only had an unending series of schisms plagued the "solidarity" of the Christian Church; it still faced active resistance and sturdy competition from the pagan religions it had never quite superseded. The Eastern and Western branches of the Church, divided over this fundamental issue of the divinity of Christ, were further divided by regional pressures and problems, decidedly nontheological in nature, which made it important from Constantinople's standpoint to, at least in principle, assert the political supremacy of Constantinople over Rome. Justinian, a theologian at heart, gave up his time to religious questions out of a love of controversy for the pure pleasure of dogmatizing. The more cosmopolitan Theodora, aware of the deep political problems that underlay the shifting and changing quarrels of the theologians, went her way unswervingly, boldly challenging the Papacy, carrying the irresolute Justinian along with her—even after her death. It was to her protection that "heretic" Egypt owed many years of toleration, and it was because of Theodora that "heretic" Syria was able to put its persecuted national church upon a firm foundation. She had always been in sympathy with the monks of Syria and Egypt, such as Zooras and Jacobus Baradeus, reciving them in the palace and entreating their prayers. It was she who made it possible for the dissenters to be restored to favor and to resume freely the spreading of their doctrines, and it was to her, more than to Justinian, that the Monophysite missions in Arabia, Nubia, and Abyssinia owed their success. A former actress, the former mistress of a provincial governor (she and Eutychius, later Patriarch at Constantinople, had formed a working relationship in those days), Theodora was concerned with only one thing—the strengthening of the State. Nothing must be allowed to stand in the way of her plans, neither God nor Man. The pretty, rather small and extraordinarily graceful woman—contemporaries talk of her face, with its pale, creamy coloring, lighted up by large, vivacious, sparkling eyes—had unquestionably been born a thousand years ahead of her time. She was a Renaissance personality with Madison Avenue expertise.

The Fifth Council was packed. Of the one hundred and sixty-five bishops present at the final meeting on June 2nd, A.D. 553, only six could in any way be described as being from the Western church—the lines were drawn that clearly by then—and their sees were located in Africa. Pope Vigilius, though originally Justinian's man, if we may use that expression, was in Constantinople throughout this period but pointedly refused to attend the sessions. As a matter of fact, it was made clear to him that he was not wanted there.

It is now known that before the opening of the Council, which had been delayed because of the resistance of the Pope, the bishops already at Constantinople were asked to consider, by order of the Emperor, a series of charges against Origenism that had nothing in common with the original teachings of Origen, but which were held by one of the so-called Origenist parties in Palestine. There is no doubt that the bishops at this extra-conciliary session subscribed to the fifteen Anathemas proposed by the Emperor (the first of which was *If anyone assert the fabulous pre-existence of souls, and shall assert the monstrous restoration which follows it, let him be anathema!*); there is no proof that the approbation of the Pope was asked. It is therefore debatable, to put it mildly, that these Anathemas were formally adopted by the Fifth Ecumenical Council, but it is not debatable that, in a masterful exercise of latter-day public relations, the world at large, and the Church of Rome, were led to believe that the teachings of Origen had been condemned. Pope Vigilius himself, Pelagius I (556–61), Pelagius II (579–90), and Gregory the Great (590–604), in treating of the Fifth Council, make no mention of Origenism and speak as if they did not know of its condemnation.

The Anathemas, which it must be pointed out were not directed solely against Origenism but were also aimed at other troublesome essentially anti-monophysite (and potentially anti-Establishment) schisms within the Eastern Church, were however a *fait accompli*.

We tend sometimes to forget the degree of sophistication and administrative competence of the machinery of state of that day. Then, as later, it was in the interest of the state, whomsoever might be Emperor, to diminish in every possible way the influence of trends, generally religious in nature, which in time could menace the *status quo*. The institution of permanent civil servants is an old one.

The lines had actually been drawn, a century earlier, and the eventual break between the Eastern and Western Churches was already a political reality (witness the composition of the Fifth Council) without being formally so acknowledged. The West thought one way, the East thought another, and this was a reality that had to be lived with, and mastered, so long as conditions in the West, coupled with the weakness, at times, of the See of Rome, left the politico-ecclesiastical initiative to Byzantium. The latter could and did, for essentially political reasons, make and unmake Popes and could force through, as at this Council, proposals which did not reflect majority thinking within the still somewhat less than united Christian world.

For a thousand years, except among essentially anti-statist schismatics such as the Cathari, the Bogomils, the Christian Gnostics and the Manicheans, the concept of pre-existence was known only to scholars. It was a matter of record, after all, that the Church had pronounced Anathema against those who professed or advocated such heresies, and with the growing authority of the Papacy, already the Church Militant in everything but name, it was dangerous, to put it mildly, to challenge those in authority.

Beginning with the Renaissance and with the Council of Florence, where the representative of the Greek Church urged Cosimo de Medici to form a Platonic Academy in Florence, there was however considerable interest at the highest levels, in spite of and possibly within the highest ranks of the Inquisition, not in Origenism as such but in the Neo-Platonist school of thought. The contribution of Muslim scholars, in Seville and Cordoba and Bagdad, to this rediscovery by the West of its past, had been immeasurable. A fantastic number of Irish and English and French and Italian monks had studied in the universities in Muslim Spain and had returned to their own schools and universities, to share what they had learned with students and other teachers. The intellectual ferment in the schools and universities in the early middle ages—instead of being as anarchic as our latter-day romantics at Columbia and at the Sorbonne would have it—resulted in speculative thinkers who, within and not outside the framework of the Establishment, were to challenge the dogma of that Establishment, strengthen and purify the Church, and initiate the reforms with which we credit the Renaissance but which actually antedated those times.

Medieval and late Medieval thinkers rediscovered Greece and Rome. Renaissance thinkers, captives like Machiavelli of a world they had not made but could only mock, contributed to what we are pleased to describe as the maturing of the West. In more recent days, the late Ananda Coomaraswamy could suggest with considerable truth that civilization, as we understood it, had taken the wrong road back in the thirteenth century.

Be this as it may, we are concerned here solely with not our sins as a race but with our virtues and among these must be included the refusal of thinkers, throughout the essentially conformist Renaissance and throughout the subsequent and basically negativist "age of enlightenment" to completely turn their backs on truths that did not have the imprimatur of the Establishment of the time.

There is for instance the long forgotten Joseph Glanvill (1636–1680), Chaplain of King Charles II, who wrote in *Lux Orientalis*, An Inquiry into the Opinions of the Eastern Sages Concerning the Praeexistence of Souls:

> "Christ and His Apostles spoke and writ as the condition of the persons, with whom they dealt, administered occasion. . . . Therefore doubtless there were many noble theories which they could have made the world acquainted with . . . Few speculative truths are delivered in Scripture but such as were called forth by the controversies of those times; and Pre-existence was none of them, it being the constant opinion of the Jews, as appears by that question, 'Master, was it for this man's sin or his father's that he was born blind?' . . . . And the author of the Book of Wisdom, who certainly was a Jew, probably Philo, plainly supposeth the same doctrine in that speech, 'For I was a witty child, and had a good spirit, wherefore . . . being good, I came into a body undefiled.'
>
> " . . . Every soul brings a kind of sense with it into the world, whereby it tastes and relisheth what is suitable to its peculiar temper. . . . What can we conclude but that the soul itself is the immediate subject of all this variety and that it came prejudiced and prepossessed into this body with some implicit notions that it had learnt in another?
>
> "To say that all this variety proceeds primarily from the mere temper of our bodies is methinks a very poor and unsatisfying account. For those that are the most like in the temper, air, and complex-

ion of their bodies, are yet of a vastly differing genius. . . . What then can we conjecture is the cause of all this diversity, but that we had taken a great delight and pleasure in some things like and analogous unto these in a former condition?"

The noted English divine, William Law (1686–1761), was even more direct in his *An Appeal to All That Doubt or Disbelieve in the Truths of the Gospel:*

"It has been an opinion commonly received, though without any Foundation in the Light of Nature, or Scripture, that God created this whole visible World and all Things in it *out of Nothing;* nay that the souls of Men and the highest Orders of Beings were created in the same Manner. The Scripture is very decisive against this Origin of the Souls of Men . . . God *breathed into Man (Spiraculum Vitarum) the Breath of Lives, and Man became a Living Soul.* Hence the Notion of a Soul created *out of Nothing* is in the plainest, strongest Manner rejected by the first Written Word of God. . . . Therefore there is in all Men, *a divine, immortal never-ending* Spirit, that can have nothing of Death in it, but *must* live forever, because it *is* the Breath of the *everliving God. . . .*"

Pre-existence was preached by the celebrated Congregational minister and reformer, Henry Ward Beecher (1813–1887), and later by Philip Brooks (1835–1893), bishop of the Episcopal Church and a noted pulpit orator in an age when this had a certain meaning. The Reverend George Foot Moore (1851–1931), Frothingham Professor of History of Religion, Harvard University, in common with William R. Inge (1860–1954), Dean of St. Paul's Cathedral, London, accepted, in principle, the doctrine not of pre-existence but of transmigration, while Dr. Paul Tillich, Professor of Theology at Harvard University, considered by many to be the foremost Protestant theologian of our time, said, in a lecture, "Symbols of Eternal Life":

"The Nirvana symbol for eternal life points to the life of absolute fullness, not to the death of absolute nothingness, as sometimes is assumed. The life of Nirvana is beyond distinction of subject and object. It is everything because it is nothing definite. . . . But in order to reach this, many reincarnations are necessary. They are continuations of temporal existence, and therefore they are considered as punishment and suffering. Only the end of temporal existence brings the full participation in eternal life. In it individualization is conquered by participation. The full recession to the ground has taken place . . . The individual is preserved, but only in its reunion with the realm of essence. . . ."

Cardinal Mercier (1851–1926), writing in *Psychologie*, said:

"Under the term *Wiedermenschwerdung*, metempsychosis, or the transmigration of souls, a great variety of ideas may be understood: either a series of repetitions of existence under the twofold condition that the soul maintains consciousness of its personality and that there is a final unit in the series of transmigrations; or a series of repetitions of existence without any final unit, and yet with the presupposition that the soul maintains consciousness of its personality; or, finally, an endless series of repetitions of existence with the loss of consciousness of personal identity . . . So far as concerns the first assumption, we do not see that reason, if left to itself, would declare this to be impossible or certainly false."

A number of Catholic priests in Poland and Italy, influenced by the mystic, Andrzej Towianski (1799–1878), be-

lieved in Reincarnation. Among these was Archbishop Passa-
valli (1820–1897) who, likewise influenced by the teachings
of Towianski, flatly stated that Reincarnation was not condemned by the Church, and that it was not at all in conflict
with any Catholic dogma. He was convinced that he had already lived many times on earth and that he was likely to return—it is worth noting that he remained Archbishop until
his death. The Catholic theologian Baron Freidrich von
Hügel, in *Essay and Addresses on the Philosophy of Religion,*
speaks of the Archbishop's "acceptance of a doctrine of
successive lives for human souls".

There are in other words precedents for the insistence,
early in this chapter, that you can be a Christian and still
believe in Reincarnation.

It is this writer's considered opinion that the Vatican
Council has pointed the way to many of us though Popes and
laymen alike have in the past, in all good faith, echoed
those all too human men and bishops who, fourteen hundred
years ago, pronounced Anathema—whether publicly or pri-
vately is by now unimportant—on this concept or doctrine of
pre-existence.

As Julius, Cardinal Dopfner, pointed out, in an address in
Munich early in 1964, there is need for new thinking. Cathol-
icism must once more be understood to be *"ecclesia semper
reformanda*—a church ever in need of reform."

> "Christ himself was free of sin; but the continua-
> tion of his work has been entrusted to frail, sinful
> humans." The Church has thus at times been guilty
> of "failing to achieve what God had desired. The
> presentation of the love of Christ can lag if the
> Church uses the means of power instead of humil-
> ity, of force instead of service."

His Eminence, obviously thinking of the days, four hundred and fifty years ago, when another German also called
for a new approach to the verities, continued:

"Even in the area of church teaching, development is far from impossible. A dogma as such is not finally synonymous with divine truth, but only incompletely expresses the wealth of divine truth because it sees revelation in human terms. This does not mean that the church can recant or change dogmatic definitions of the past, but it can discover new aspects of truth, and find new ways to express traditional teaching."

Yes, assuming your understanding of Christianity is broad enough and rich enough, you can accept the doctrine of the pre-existence of the Soul.

Others have done so, long, long ago.

Others will do so, in the Days After Tomorrow, assuming the Race be granted those Days.

VI

HYPNOTISM AND REINCARNATION

Can you be induced, while under hypnosis, to "remember" your past lives?

Yes.

And also no.

The difficulty lies in the fact that the widespread interest in the answer to this question has prompted experiments—by amateur hypnotists, well-meaning physicians untrained in this application of hypnosis, psychologists and laymen, and also by charlatans and adventurers professing to be both initiates and hypnotists—which not only have added nothing to our understanding of this potentiality of the Inner Self, but have instead confused matters still further, thoroughly muddying the waters.

Metaphysically oriented circles are the happy hunting grounds of charlatans and adventurers who, though inadequately trained, profess an incidental mastery over forces normally attained only after years of discipline (psychic and otherwise) to which these gentlemen are normally alien. We know, you and I know, that there is no easy road to True Understanding. You cannot approach these matters after cocktails, or while between husbands, or for that matter in between lovers. You must be prepared to surrender yourself, body and soul, to study and meditation, and this is seldom if ever possible under the conditions of life known to most of us.

Our society does not permit us to pause.

Or to meditate.

Or to search within ourselves for the Understanding which we at times sense can be found there.

There is no escape, for most of us, from the world around us, and if we therefore subject ourselves to disciplines taught us by men who themselves have not lived by them, we run the risk of damaging our bodies and our minds—particularly our minds.

Performing Yogic exercises forty-five minutes a day by the clock and then turning, with a sigh, to the normal demands life makes upon you, is not enough to restore either Youth or Love. Or both.

At a certain stage in your life, particularly if in previous lives you have had some experience of and have subordinated yourself to these disciplines, meditation and a study of these schools of thought, which ante-date our Judeo-Christian approach to infinity, will obviously help you to live through these days and to endure these times.

But it cannot be stressed too strongly and it cannot be repeated too often that there is no easy road to Understanding.

And there is no easy road to Initiatehood.

A number of self-styled Mystery Schools will promise you mastery of the forces within you, assuming you pass through a series of preliminary steps, pay the necessary fees, study and, at least in principle, master the Teachings you are told the Masters handed down to those who now instruct you, in the flesh or through the printed word. Ascended Master Jesus Christ, not to mention other Ascended Masters—there are a number of them to be found in the quasi-metaphysical calendar—will in the main do no particular harm to either your body or to your mind so long as what is demanded of you is adherence to and a modicum of understanding of Truths actually taught by no one Teacher, but by many Teachers, or for that matter by no single *ancient* Mystery School, but by many.

Where the danger lies is when you get into the hands of a man, himself inadequately trained, who imposes upon you disciplines which he himself does not understand, or who meddles with forces which, ineptly evoked or even more ineptly controlled, can cause you to withdraw into a world of shadows known only to you and understood only by you, and peopled both by your memories and by your fears, and by your waking dreams.

Putting yourself into the hands of an untrained hypnotist, who may be a sort of metaphysical voyeur, can be equally dangerous—particularly if the hypnotist has a strong personality and the ability to influence, whether consciously or otherwise (I lean over backwards in saying so), your memories of your own past. While it may be comforting to learn that you have been Akhenaton (and chances are that you do not know that this is a distinction shared by many), the danger lies in the possibility that the hypnotist, howevermuch he may try, cannot completely bring you out of this hypnotically induced fantasy world. You thus find yourself, in addition to your certainty that you possess knowledge vouchsafed to few, living simultaneously in two coexistent and equally real worlds. If, in addition to this, you have over the years convinced yourself, and possibly others, that something happened to you as the result of alien intelligences contacting you, telepathically or otherwise, then, to put it mildly, life becomes infinitely complicated, both for those who love you and for those who believe in you.

In other times, there were simpler and more predictable reactions to such accounts, howevermuch truth there may have been to them, or however mad the tellers of these tales may have obviously been. It was clear that you were possessed by the Devil, and various and properly blessed corrective measures needed to be taken, including burning you at the stake, after the mandatory torture to discover who else, or whom else, you might have influenced to the ways of Satan.

In these more complex times, in which we take a certain gloomy pride in knowing as little as possible about our past, and dismiss as science fiction any consideration of our possible Tomorrows, we do not burn the Strange and the Alien.

No. We either lock them up, obviously for their own good, or we do something almost worse, we laugh at them, and dismiss them as crackpots, pleasantly mad, and, of course, harmless. Ours is a generation that has developed, almost to the extent of establishing it as a new science, this ability to dismiss or to denigrate that which we do not understand. It is simpler and considerably less taxing on everyone concerned to do so.

As a result we leave these people to the tender mercies of the charlatans and the emotional blackmailers, that peculiarly talented fringe element within metaphysically oriented circles who thrive on the exploitation of fears and on the lemming-like search for reassurance of the many who seek from life things which are alien to their contemporaries.

Because acceptance of the concept of pre-existence is equally misunderstood in our society, men such as these are allowed to exploit those who search for understanding. It is these gentlemen I've had in mind in what I've just said, and not the properly qualified researchers in the paranormal sciences, whose work I propose to discuss in due course.

In at this time first considering the Bridey Murphy case, and then proceeding to discuss another and a sounder approach to the directing of the memory of a person, under hypnosis, to recall or relive past lives, I do not of course mean to suggest that Morey Bernstein, the hypnotist involved and author of *The Search for Bridey Murphy* (1956, Doubleday), is one of these gentlemen of doubtful virtue whom I have just excoriated. Certainly not.

I am afraid however that the old saw about fools who rush in where angels fear to tred does come to mind when you consider men such as this.

I am inclined to prefer the adventurer, whether self-taught or unfrocked, who at least has some understanding of the forces with which he is meddling, to the amateur, however well-meaning, however sincere, however honest and however pure-in-heart, at least for the moment, who can do such irreparable harm to his student or to his subject, if he be a hypnotist, because of his "bull in a china shop" approach and because of his failure to understand that our minds are delicate things into which you may not probe with single-minded Rotarian heartiness.

Morey Bernstein, a late convert to hypnotism and, almost to the Moment of Truth, a sceptic on this subject of Reincarnation, was treading on dangerous ground as he went beyond the act or induction of hypnosis and began, in effect, to probe into his subject's emotional life. He wasn't qualified to take these chances with the mind of his subject, because it is obvious that the mere induction of hypnosis may interfere with the very sensitive balance of the subject's emotional defenses and set up a storm—'fet up a breeze, as West Indians put it —even a psychotic one. The radio broadcasts of the tape recordings of Bernstein's experiments revealed the disturbing anxiety to which his subject was exposed; the subject was under tremendous emotional strain, a situation which the hypnotist should have been on the *qui vive* for, instead of half ignoring. . . . There is no room for brinkmanship when one is probing into the human mind!

Bernstein's subject, a young woman called "Ruth Simmons", had lived in Belfast during the first half of the 19th century, in this former life of hers, and in successive sessions, as she was questioned by Bernstein, she ranged back and forth over her years in Cork and in Belfast, and also in her life in the astral world.

Bernstein asks if there was anything in that astral world— that half-way house between one life and the next—which could be described as death, disease, or old age. Just to be sure that she does not misunderstand him he repeats himself —"Were there any such things as death, disease, or old age in that astral world?"

The answer is immediate. "There was no death, there was just a . . . passing of . . . you passed from that existence . . . you passed . . . to another existence. That's all, there was no death."

There was no disease. There was no old age. She did not get older than the sixty-six she had been when she died. There were no laws, no regulations—you just went where you willed to go, as Bernstein put it somewhat incredulously

—you did what you willed to do. . . . It is worth noting that to each question, at this stage, the subject just answers, "No." *

As one man, not identified by Bernstein, pointed out, men had for years been trying to learn whether man's consciousness survives the death of his physical body. There had been repeated attempts to establish some sort of communication after the death of the physical body. Experiments such as Bernstein's suggested the possibility of reversing the direction of these investigations and of instead establishing evidence of individual consciousness *before* birth.**

There is a certain naive ruthlessness about these part-time researchers—Bernstein is not the only one after all, he was only more publicity-and-promotion conscious—which is disturbing and even distressing if you have something of the sensitive in you, and I use the word now in its metaphysical sense.

This is perhaps ridiculous in an age of capsulated wisdom, where a pill can mean either death or life, or understanding or the opposite of understanding, according to the metabolism, psychic and otherwise, of the person involved.

It cannot be too strongly stressed however that if the hypnotist is ignorant of (or insensitive to) the true nature of the inter-relationship between subject and hypnotist, he can begin to have trouble with his subject who, as "Ruth Simmons" did at one stage, can show evidence of deeply resenting the hypnotist's pressure, his probings, and his attempts to "verify" previous statements, possible only if you are dealing, at least in theory, with a more sophisticated memory. The subject, though supposedly under deep hypnosis, now tries to defend herself, as "Ruth Simmons" did at one stage, instead of being the passive receptive typical hypnotic subject. She becomes irritable and annoyed at questions which, all too obviously,

* Bernstein, pps. 147–48.
** ibid, pps. 209–10.

reflect the questioner's lack of understanding, to put it mildly, of the matters under discussion.

There is no suggestion here though of what we may describe as hypnotically induced pseudo-memories. This is still another problem and a very serious problem though there is no doubt that no particular damage is done to that man or that woman who is convinced, after a series of sessions, that he or she are the reincarnations of Joan of Arc, Tutankhamon, George Washington, or of others who contributed to the history of their times. The many incarnations of Akhnaton are unlikely to meet, in their time, and each will live out their years in blessed unawareness of the other.

This is not the problem here. There is no reason to doubt the Bridey Murphy story. "Ruth Simmons" undoubtedly had lived in Belfast in an earlier life, and to dismiss the entire story as fantasy, as some critics predictably rushed to do, was a reaction founded on these critics' prejudices rather than objectivity. Bernstein can be faulted on the score of not so much ineptness as not yet fully knowing his tools.

With this in mind it is doubly important to approach this matter of the inter-relationship of hypnotism and the awareness of former lives, not as a parlor game, not as something bizarre, not as a palliative, but as a way in which we may in time, if we exercise care, learn more about ourselves, and perhaps even about the dim Tomorrows.

No study of the role of hypnotism in our search for knowledge of our past lives would be complete if we did not at this moment pause to discuss at some length the contribution to this question of the late Edgar Cayce who, while still a child in Kentucky, displayed powers of perception extending beyond the normal range of the five senses. When Edgar Cayce died, in January, 1945, in Virginia Beach, Virginia, he left more than fourteen thousand documented stenographic records of the telepathic-clairvoyant statements or readings he had given for more than six thousand people over a period of forty-three years. These documents, as his son Hugh Lynn Cayce has pointed out, "constitute one of the largest and most impressive records of psychic perception ever to emanate from a single individual." This material, together with relevant records, correspondence and reports, is at the disposal of the serious-minded students and investigators who continue to come to Virginia Beach to examine these records which have been gathered together by the Association for Research and Enlightenment, Inc., better known as A.R.E., headed by Hugh Lynn Cayce.

In twenty-five hundred readings given between 1925 and 1944, Edgar Cayce was concerned with psychological problems examined by him in the light of what he termed the "karmic patterns" arising out of previous lives spent by the individual soul on this earth. Karma, as he saw it, was a universal law of cause and effect which provides the soul with repeated opportunities for physical, mental and spiritual growth. Each soul, called an "Entity" by Cayce, as it reenters the earthplane, has subconscious access to the characteristics, mental capacities and skills it may have accumulated in previous lives. At the same time the Entity must also cope with the influence on the present life of former lives in which they had yielded, to put it mildly, to hate and fear and cruelty and greed. The Entity's task on earth, to quote Hugh Lynn Cayce, "is to make use of its successive rebirths to balance its positive and negative karmic patterns by subduing its selfish impulses and encouraging its creative urges." *

It all started, in August of 1923, in a hotel room in Dayton, Ohio, when Edgar Cayce had woken from a self-imposed hypnotic sleep to receive what must have been one of the greatest shocks of his life.

It must be remembered that Cayce was a devout and orthodox Protestant. His education had been confined to a literal acceptance of the Bible. He had accepted it verbatim and taught it verbatim in Sunday School and read the Bible through, year after year, drawing total spiritual comfort from this rigid and unyielding interpretation of Truth, as he under-

---

* Hugh Lynn Cayce in his introduction to Noel Langley's EDGAR CAYCE ON REINCARNATION.

stood it to be. Until that moment there had been no doubt in his mind that this was not Revealed Truth.

But at that moment, as the stenographer read back what Cayce had said, he learned that he had stated flatly that Reincarnation was not an impious myth but very, very real.

His first reaction, an understandable one, was that he had been taken over, while in his trance, by the Forces of Evil. He had always said that if his powers were to thus, in a sense, play him false, he would permit no further use of these powers which God had given him. He was a troubled man that day when an admittedly new concept of Reincarnation first came about, a concept which neither challenged nor impugned the teachings of Christ but laid the foundation for an approach, a spiritual philosophy, of particular interest to those Christians who, each in his way, had come to share the belief of the early Church Fathers in pre-existence or rebirth.

In the years that followed it was increasingly clear that the only God the sleeping Edgar Cayce "knew" was not the angry God of the fundamentalists but "a loving God of infinite mercy" who had already forgiven His children. We are not concerned here, however, with the extent to which the waking man may in fact have influenced the sleeping man—it is clear that he did so, but on this occasion this is not important.

What is important is that this man helped and healed thousands.

And, as this happened, these people also learned about themselves, why they did what they did, and what might happen to them in the course of time.

In a talk he gave at the Cayce Hospital in 1931 Edgar Cayce described how on one occasion, on going into the unconscious state to obtain information for an individual, he realized that he was leaving his body.

"There was just a direct, straight, and narrow line in front of me, like a shaft of white light. On either side was fog and smoke, and many shadowy figures who seemed to be crying to me for help, and begging me to come aside to the plane they occupied.

"As I followed along the shaft of light, the way began to clear. The figures on either side grew more distinct; they took on clearer form. But there was a continual beckoning back, or the attempt to sidetrack me and bring me aside from my purpose. Yet with the narrow way in front of me, I kept going straight ahead. After a while I passed to where the figures were merely shadows attempting to urge me on, rather than to stop me. As they took on more form, they seemed to be occupied with their own activities.

"Finally I came to a hill, where there was a mount and a temple. I entered this temple and found in it a very large room, very much like a library. Here were the books of people's lives, for each person's activities were a matter of actual record, it seemed. And I merely had to pull down the record of the individual for whom I was seeking information. I have to say as Paul did, 'Whether I was in the spirit or out of the spirit, I cannot tell'; but that was an actual experience." *

There is compassion and concern as Edgar Cayce, howsomever he may have attained the knowledge, traced the lives of those who came to him for a Life Reading. In life after life, though often at seemingly greater intervals than we are told of by others, they had at times known each other, loved each other, or fought each other, as far back as in Egypt of 10,000 B.C., or longer ago.

The sister-in-law of one subject had been a close friend of this subject in Nero's Rome, but had been denounced by her as a secret Christian—the two girls were in love with the same man—and she had met her death in the arena. In prehistoric Egypt she had developed the talent for nursing which had enabled her to care for her sister-in-law in this life, but in

* Langley, pps. 46–47.

a later life in Arabia she had been vain and jealous of her social position, and resentful when age had forced her into the background. In the Roman period, converted by Paul himself at the secret meetings in the catacombs, she died forgiving the friend who had denounced her. But in her next life she had played a role in the French Revolution where for a time she was in a position of influence, perhaps not a Madame Tallien, more likely, since in time the Revolution destroyed her, still another Madame Defarge.

"As you do unto others . . ." A young man who had been a member of the French Court in the days of Louis XVI had been merciless as he ridiculed the homosexuals at Court. In this life he found himself struggling against this same compulsion.

In an earlier incarnation a woman in her early thirties, a compulsive drinker and a nymphomaniac, had been a king's daughter who had not hesitated to sit in judgement over women weaker than herself, leaving little if any room for tolerance or pity in her single-minded self-righteousness. She had finally retired to a convent in order to avoid further "contamination" by those around her.

The influence of past lives upon the present, if it can be phrased this way, is illustrated in the case of the much married psychologist who found himself, as the war ended, in charge of a school were men were being trained to drop behind enemy lines, located on the same spot on Long Island where in an earlier life, as a British staff officer, he had mapped and laid out the plans of Howe and Clinton against Washington's forces.

In marked contrast to the preceding Reading, which had to do with a man who had also been a voluptuary—and something of a scientist—in an earlier incarnation in Persia, there is this Life Reading given a three-year-old child in 1936.*

"Much crowds in to be said, for the Entity is very sensitive, very high-strung, inclined to be very

* Langley, p. 99.

stubborn, and very expressive of feeling. . . . For the Entity is an old soul, and an Atlantean who, properly guided and directed, may not only make for his own development but make his surroundings, his environs, his world, a much better place for others.

"It will be found that few people will appear as strangers to the Entity, yet some will remain strangers ever, no matter how often or in what manner they are thrown together! The Entity will ever be tending towards an idealistic nature. Hence, unless it be made clear to the Entity as to why there will be faults and failures in the promises made by individuals and associates, he will tend to lose confidence, not only in others, but in self.

"And the loneliest person, the loneliest individual, yea the loneliest Entity, is the one who has lost hold upon his own self!"

Cayce warned that the child would continuously seek new fields of activity, "for everything about the Entity must be new." The Entity had been a Roman official and, still earlier, during the last days of Atlantis, he had been an official responsible for the emigration of the people to settlements in Egypt, the Pyrenees, and Central and South America. His father had been with him in past lives, including the life in Egypt, at the time of the Exodus. In that same incarnation his mother had been his daughter, and Cayce warned that there would be times when he would doubt his parent's authority.

What was to be the boy's vocation? Cayce suggested law, preferably international law.

What we have been in past lives, while able to influence the present, need have nothing to do with the way we manage our present lives. We are influenced, or more properly influencable, by the past, but we cannot take refuge in it and ignore our primary responsibility to make what we can of our present existence.

Cayce made this very clear in his Reading of a twelve-year-old boy whose mother was bewildered by what is gently described as "his mercurial behavior-pattern".*

"In giving the records here of this Entity, it would be easy to interpret them either in a very optimistic or a very pessimistic vein. For there are great possibilities and great obstacles. Here is the opportunity for an Entity (while comparisons are odious, these would be good comparisons) to be either a Beethoven or a Whittier; or a Jesse James! For the Entity is inclined to think more highly of himself than he ought; and that is what these three individuals did. As to the application made of it, this depends upon the individual self.

"Here is an Entity who has abilities latent within self which may be turned into music, or poetry, or writing in prose which few would ever excel. Or there may be the desire to have his own way to such an extent that he will disregard others altogether, in every form, just so he has his own way.

"In giving the astrological aspects, these are latent and manifested: Mercury, Venus, Jupiter, Saturn and Mars. These are adverse in some respects, one to another, yet are ever present, and indicate that the body will go to excess in many ways, unless there is real training in the period of unfoldment. And the Entity is beginning to reach that period when—while the spirit must not be broken!—everyone should be very firm and positive, inducing him through reason to analyze himself, and to form a proper concept of his ideals and purposes, and in doing this, we will not only give the world a real individual with genius, but make for proper soul development. Otherwise, we will give to the world one with a genius for making trouble for somebody!"

* Langley, p. 117.

Somewhere—somehow—the parents failed with this child, possibly by reason of their own inability to fully understand, inwardly, the problems involved. Edgar Cayce had talked of the need for firm and positive guidance, but this is often a delegated responsibility in an age and in a society where parents, particularly when they can afford to do so, pay others to do what they should themselves do. The teacher becomes a substitute parent. If then the teacher is inadequate, trouble can ensue.

What distinguishes Edgar Cayce from others who likewise claim access to the Akashic Records is this stern and uncompromising refusal to in the main do anything more than, in the vernacular of today's youth, "to tell it like it is." It is clear that Cayce regarded himself as a channel—as a channel for healing and as a channel for understanding—and nothing more than this. His own attitude to his psychic power is reflected in a talk he gave to the A.R.E. in 1933.*

"As to the validity of the information which comes through me when I sleep—this is the question, naturally, that occurs to everyone. Personally I feel that its validity depends largely upon how much faith and confidence lie within the one who seeks this source of information.

"In regard to this same source of information, even though I have been doing this work for thirty-one years, I know very little about it. Whatever I might say would be largely a matter of conjecture. I can make no claims whatsoever to great knowledge, for I also am only groping.

"But then, we all learn by experience, do we not? We come to have faith and understanding only by taking one step at a time. Most of us don't have the experience of getting religion all at once, like the man who got it halfway between the bottom of the well and the top, when he was blown out by an explosion of dynamite! Most of us need to arrive at

* Langley, pps. 143-144.

our conclusions by weighing the evidence along with something that answers from deep within our inner selves.

"As a matter of fact, there would seem to be not just one, but several sources of information tapped when I am in this sleeping state.

"One source, apparently, is the record made by an individual in all of its experiences through what we call time. The sum total of the experiences of that soul is written, so to speak, in the subconscious of that individual as well as in what is known as the Akashic Records. Anyone may read these records, if he can attune himself rightly. Apparently I am one of the few people who may lay aside the personality sufficiently to allow the soul to make this attunement to the universal source of knowledge. I say this, however, not in a boastful way; in fact, I don't claim to possess any power that any other person doesn't possess. I sincerely believe that there isn't any person, anywhere, who doesn't have the same ability I have. I'm certain that all human beings have much greater powers than they are ever aware of—provided they are willing to pay the price of detachment from self-interest which is required to develop those powers or abilities. Would you be willing, even once a year, to put aside your own personality—to pass entirely away from it?

"Many people ask me how I prevent undesirable influences from entering into the work I do. In order to answer that question, let me tell an experience I had when I was a child. When I was between eleven and twelve years of age, I had read the Bible three times. Now I have read it fifty-six times. No doubt some people have read it more times than that. But I have tried to read it once for each year of my life.

"Well, as a child, I prayed that I might be able to do something for other people—to aid them in understanding themselves, and especially to aid children in their ills. One day I had a vision which convinced me that my prayer had been heard and would be answered.

"So I believe that my prayer is still being answered. And as I go into the unconscious condition, I do so with that faith. I also believe that the source of information will be from the Universal, if the connection is not made to waver by the desires of the person seeking the Reading."

We have here then a Christian mystic—Protestantism, particularly American Protestantism, has had its share of these —who has, in his own way, approached this question which we have considered elsewhere of whether the acceptance of pre-existence, or rather Reincarnation, is reconcilable with a belief in the Christ.

Edgar Cayce, as a Christian and as a psychic, approached this question with both the limitations and the strength of a Man of Faith—limitations because inevitably his would be an unconsciously subjective approach to the question—strength because a Man of Faith, irrespective of what that Faith may be, approaches a question like this not as a dilettante, not as an intellectual *voyeur*, but as a man who has implicit faith in the God Force which he considers incontrovertible.

While we may therefore question not what he "saw" but perhaps at times his interpretation of what he "saw", we can respect the obvious integrity of the man who, in a talk in 1931, asked: *

"What is life? What is this phenomenon of life? Where and how do the various phenomena manifest themselves?

"We have a physical body; we have a mental body; we have a spiritual body, or soul. Now each of these has its own attributes. Just as the physical body has divisions—all dependent one upon the

* Langley, pps. 145–146.

other, and some more dependent than the rest—so
the mind has its own source of activity that mani-
fests in various ways through the individual body.

"The soul also has its attributes, and its various
ways of gaining, maintaining or manifesting itself
among men. The pyschic force is a manifestation of
the soul mind."

Still another, and perhaps the most interesting, approach to
the role of hypnotism in our search for knowledge of our
past lives is that of Joan Grant and her husband, Denys Kelsey, M.B.,M.R.C.P., an analytically oriented psychiatrist who
had come to a belief in Reincarnation through clinical evidence accumulating during the ten years prior to his first
meeting Joan Grant.

Almost immediately after being asked to temporarily take
over for the medical officer in the psychiatric wing of the
military hospital with which he was connected, a series of
cases had come Dr. Kelsey's way which, step by step, in a
sense extended the framework of what he could accept as
fact. After four years a session with one particular patient
forced him (the phrase is his own) to "the intellectual certainty that in a human being there is a component which is
not physical." * He had been using hypnosis as, if we may
phrase it this way, a medical tool, in marked contrast to those
who still only saw and see it as parlor entertainment.

Dr. Kelsey was concerned professionally not so much with
the preconscious storage-house of every memory, every item
of knowledge, that the patient has accumulated over his lifetime, but with the so-called unconscious part of the mind
(the hardest and the most dangerous to penetrate if the hypnotist is inexperienced) where these less easily categorizable
memories and impulses also exist, or are stored.

While hypnosis is generally spoken of as sleep, this is not
necessarily accurate. "Indeed", as Dr. Kelsey points out,**

* Kelsey 25.
** Ibid, p. 28.

"unless a specific suggestion is made to the contrary, a person under hypnosis may be unusually wide awake, in the sense that his powers of perception may be abnormally acute. But since such a person is not in a state of normal-waking-consciousness, perhaps the best description of hypnosis is 'a state of altered consciousness.' An important feature of this state is that it weakens the barrier which confines the contents of the unconscious. This can be of particular value in psychiatry because it may enable the therapist to bring material from the patient's unconscious to the surface more quickly than would otherwise be possible."

Dr. Kelsey, once back in civil life, took a post in a mental hospital where he remained for the next six years. During that time he increasingly came to recognize that the memory of an event, including the sensations and emotions associated with it, could be stored in either the preconscious or the unconscious. If stored in the preconscious, from which it could readily be summoned to consciousness, it was obviously a part of the total experience upon which the individual could, consciously or otherwise, base future decisions. If however these memories had been forced into the unconscious, prompting seemingly irrational feelings and behavior, the hypno-therapist, probing into the subject's mind, could determine the reason for such behavior—at times traceable to something which may have happened when the subject was very young—and help the patient towards recovery.

Regression under hypnosis is an extension of those moments when we find ourselves not only remembering but living in the past. For a brief while, perhaps only for a moment, we seem to be in that past—there are the smells, the laughter, the tears, the sense of wonder, which we associate with that long gone past. Regression under hypnosis, when performed under clinically controlled conditions and not by an amateur hypnotist, can represent a longer visit to that past, to that childhood, to the first years of that childhood, to the moment of birth, and to the prior months of intra-uterine life.

And before this life . . .

Implicit in this recognition of Reincarnation is the realization that what Joan Grant calls the supra-physical body does not die. It consists of an order of matter, molecules if you wish, which is not subject to the process we call "death," a process during which the physical particles integrated by an energy-field have become inactive. The current personality does not die; it is one of a series of personalities and essentially immortal. It is the body, the chemical makeup of which we all learn at school—the host body, if we may term it that way—that "dies".

That which has dwelt in that body, on the other hand, cannot and does not die.

This awareness of the fact that we have in effect two bodies, the physical and the supra-physical (in contradistinction to Cayce's approach), is far from new.

This is something that was accepted as a matter of course in more metaphysically enlightened civilizations, such as that of early dynastic Egypt, and for that matter throughout the first centuries of the Christian faith.

The politically oriented Fifth Ecumenical Council, convened in the sixth century by the Byzantine Emperor Justinian, undoubtedly did take a stand, though apparently *in camera,* against this school of thought which it so happened represented a menace (testimony to its strength!) to the Establishment of the day. Later, so-called schismatics within Christianity have, time and time again, throughout the Middle Ages and the Renaissance and through to our times, kept alive, even within Christianity, this older approach to what we are.

The dogmatists, who could not accept a nonmaterial reality —in the sixth century, like in the sixteenth century, like in the twentieth century, there were "realists" who doubted that which they could not see or touch or themselves experience —confused the supra-physical with the physical body.

The result has been chaos—doctrinal as well as medical— to the detriment of our lives and of our health. We have forgotten that the physical body has no reality except in the immediate present, for today's "version" of that physical body has in a sense replaced yesterday's, which has therefore ceased to exist. This however does not apply to earlier versions of that body's supra-physical component. These supra-physical components, immune to the process of what we know as death, can maintain an independent identity so long as the personality provides them with sufficient energy, using the word in its higher sense, to do so.

As a matter of fact, it is unusual to find an individual in whom several supra-physicals do not co-exist. Multiple supra-physicals can be a valuable asset to the personality, providing it not only with a wider field of activity, but also facilitating identification with people of different age or social groups.

Here is a possible explanation for those who are capable of seemingly being all things to all men, close to suspect in our filing-card-minded society where, in a fascinating carryover from nineteenth century thinking, you do not empathize with those outside your immediate circle.

These multiple supra-physicals have been compared to a wardrobe full of clothes which are available for any appropriate occasion. Where trouble sets in is when any of them contains an undue amount of energy that it cannot or will not release or channel. This energy can then cause trouble to the rest of the current personality, making for what is at times dismissed as an uncoordinated mind. Or body.

Extrapolating from this concept of the supra-physical body, we have a credible rationale for what is generally called "Spiritual Healing".

"In this connection", as Dr. Kelsey points out,* "the supra-physical may be likened to a magnet that is placed beneath a sheet of paper upon which have been scattered some iron filings. The lines of force traveling between one end of the magnet and the other will draw the filings into a definite pattern and hold them there. Similarly, the energy of the supra-physical maintains the particles which make up the physical body in a definite pattern, but one of function as well as

* Kelsey, pps. 81–82.

structure. Disease or injury disturb this pattern, and healing represents the efforts of the supra-physical to bring it back to normal. Medicine and surgery in the ordinary sense concentrate on trying to minimize the task which the supra-physical has to perform: perhaps by remedying a lack of some vitamin or hormone or other essential substance; perhaps by giving a drug that makes it impossible for bacteria to proliferate; perhaps by excising a tumour or by fixing some injured part in the position most favorable for healing to occur. But it would seem a rational procedure also to supplement the energy in the supra-physical and I think there is considerable evidence to suggest that this is possible."

What does the Healer do? Under certain circumstances he, physically contacting the affected area, concentrating first on making a vivid mental picture of the anatomy of the affected area, asks the subject to let the pain flow into the Healer's hand so that it can be thrown away, after which the Healer visualizes himself driving energy into the affected area in order to hasten the healing.

There is no denying that cases such as these, not to mention more dramatic instances of Healing, carry no scientific weight whatever. Ours is a materialistic society. At the same time, such acts—and innumerable therapists and still more Healers tell substantially the same story—would appear to support rather than detract from the validity of the concept of transferring energy to the superphysical body.

What is demanded of the therapist, and the qualified investigator, is to understand that there are levels of reality other than the one which can be perceived through the known five senses. There is in fact reason to believe that there are laws (not of the *Lex* Justinian variety!) which govern both the transmission and the reception of the energy involved in healing.

Faith enters into it obviously—an almost atavistic faith on the part of the subject in the efficacy of the act of healing—but what we have to face is the reality that there's more to it than that. The Healer unquestionably draws upon an inner strength—Edgar Cayce did it, others have done it—which cannot be defined materially because, if I may put it this way, it is *above* matter.

The concept of the supra-physical body, in its strength and in its possible complexity as a distinct element of the personality either in need of healing or of understanding, is obviously important to an understanding of Reincarnation.

The two problems are at times one. A fear, apparently irrational, can be traced to an experience in a past life, or to a negative act of the Entity, to borrow Edgar Cayce's expression for a moment, which is now having its karmic effect upon the subject.

One question can be asked with obvious validity—can every subject who is able to reach a deep state of hypnosis (keep in mind that this is not necessarily synonymous with hypnotically induced sleep) be regressed to an earlier lifetime?

The need to explore an earlier lifetime does not always arise and, only on occasion, will it be possible for the subject to recall a single episode. Even when the subject accepts the concept of Reincarnation and only seeks evidence of personal continuity, the hypnotist cannot always help him to gain it.

A number of factors can, as a matter of fact, invalidate some claims to far-memory, to here use Joan Grant's term for it. The subject may recover an episode which appears to be plausible, although in fact it has become grossly distorted "in transit" to his or her present consciousness. This may stem from the subject's desire, consciously or otherwise, to delude or impress. It is widely held that patients tend to produce the type of material that will please the psychiatrist, and this is undoubtedly true in certain rather publicised instances where subjects under hypnosis have had an almost (and incredible) total recall. The problem there is where to fix the responsibility and there are times when there is reason to believe that the hypnotist, consciously or otherwise, has unduly influenced the subject, particularly in instances of unusually detailed "memories".

What is needed is therefore not blind (and bland) acceptance of what you are being told, but an awareness of the need for closely examining the story, or more often the vignette, the isolated happening, described by the subject under hypnosis.

Here is as good a time as any to touch on a related phenomenon referred to at times in ufological and of course also metaphysically minded circles.

For one or another reason you may be able to concentrate on someone in another location, and appear to visit that person and to talk to that person and to counsel that person even though you are in actuality miles away.

What that other person sees is not a ghost.

A ghost is a dissociated fragment of a personality that has become split off from the rest and remains imprisoned in a timeless present.

What that other person sees is you, an aspect of your integrated self which, acting independently of your physical body, has been able to condense sufficiently to appear substantial.

No. I do not digress. But this is a subject which deserves fuller treatment than the scope of the present book permits.

VII

MEMORIES

We come now to what the cynical will be inclined to dismiss as the folklore of Reincarnation, ignoring the reality that it is through the folklore of a people, as through the *mythos* of a faith, that we can begin to understand what has happened in the long ago.

Dreams play their role in these stories—dreams which you can no doubt explain away if you subscribe to the Freudian tenet that dream symbols (an expression which includes a multitude of things) can be reduced to a very simple alphabet of symbolism.

This may be true, but the trouble is that we are not talking about that kind of dream. We are not scurrying around in the inner recesses of the mind, or those that seem inner to us, hunting for pleasantly titillating items of Freudian mumbo-jumbo.

We are instead concerned with the distinct possibility that while we are absent from our physical body, or in a state where our inner Self can more easily reach us, we can be in receipt of messages from someone we know to be dead at the moment of "talking" to them. Someone you have loved or been close to can try to convince you that he is alive again. Or tell you something that he knows, which you cannot possibly know.

Or tell you, as a five-year-old child attempted to tell her grieving mother in Sicily in 1910, that she would come back to her, that she would be little again, and the child made motions with her arms pantomiming the holding of a small body.

The mother couldn't believe it at first. The father, a doctor and a sceptic, obviously blamed grief over the dead child for the fantasies his wife was having, particularly when she insisted that she would soon bear twin girls. Pregnancy was out of the question for the woman, medically out of the question!

And still she gave birth to twins.

And one of the twins resembled the dead child to a disturbing extent, both physically and psychologically. The newborn child had the idiosyncracies of the child that had passed on. Like her, she was always anxious that her little hands be clean and would insist on having them washed if they were in the least degree dirty. And like the other child, she'd show a singular dislike for cheese and wouldn't even touch soup if it had a taste of cheese in it. Even her ways of playing were the same as the other child's.

When the girl was eight, the parents told the twins that the family was planning an excursion to a nearby town. The girl protested that she knew the town and had already seen the sights there and when the mother insisted she must be confusing it with another place, the girl protested that this wasn't so and began to describe incidents which had happened when the family had visited the town ten years before, just before the other child's death.

In still another case the mother also dreamt that her deceased child told her she was coming back, and she insisted to her husband that she had heard the girl's familiar voice tell her she was returning to them.

Nine years after the death of the first girl, when the new child, named for her dead sister, was six years old, the startled parents heard her sing a lullaby which the deceased child had loved. The parents had deliberately blotted out all recollection of the tune from their minds; the memories evoked by it were too painful.

And still there the child was singing this song.

The mother asked, hesitantly, what she was singing.

A French song, the child answered.

Who had taught her such a pretty song, the father broke in.

Nobody, the child shrugged. She just knew it out of her own head.

There is the case of the dying woman who told her closest friend that she would come back as her daughter, and ten months after she had died, her friend did give birth to a daughter.

When the little girl was two and a half years old, she began to recall events in her former life. Over a period of years she made more than one hundred statements about this former life, each of them recorded and verified by her father, and gradually the other children (children being normally more matter-of-fact about these matters than their parents) were aware of the fact that this sister of theirs had apparently known some of them before she was born. So? You can almost see the shrugged shoulders. She was particularly fond of an older brother and would protest when she thought he was being mistreated. When they asked her why she felt so protective towards him, she reminded them that she had been his godmother in her former life.

There is the case of the Tlingit family in south-eastern Alaska where the son insisted one day that grandfather's watch belonged to him. It was *his* watch, the five-year-old boy insisted.

The grandfather had been a well-known Alaskan fisherman, a healthy, robust man, always active, who like his fellow Tlingits had believed in Reincarnation. When he was out fishing with his son the older man would often tell him that if there really was anything to the idea, he would come back as his son. Ignoring the protestations of the young people, he'd tell them that he would be reborn with the same birthmarks as he presently bore, and on one occasion, shortly before his death, he handed his watch to his son, telling him to take good care of it until he came back to reclaim it.

Nine months after his death his daughter-in-law went into labor. As she lay in the delivery room waiting for the anaesthetic to take effect, she thought she saw her father-in-law standing by her bedside, and when she came out of the anaesthetic she fully expected to see him still there in the room. Instead she was introduced to her son, who had been born with moles precisely in the same places as those on his grandfather's body.

As the boy began to grow up, his behavior traits, his likes and dislikes and skills, were seen to coincide exactly with those of his grandfather. Even the way he walked, from his first faltering steps, was like the way his grandfather had walked. He not only looked like him, and behaved like him, but also worried like him. As far as he was concerned, his uncles and his aunts were his sons and daughters. As some might put it, he was in many ways old for his years, so much so that his brothers and sisters would call him "grandpa". He didn't mind. He knew they were right.

There is the Ceylonese boy who at the age of two revealed an extraordinarily detailed knowledge of a past life and a past crime, the details of which he could not possibly have known. He was muttering to himself about his arm being deformed because he had murdered his wife in his former life. All his mother knew was that her husband had once commented on the similarities between the boy and his deceased brother, and once even said, "This is my brother come back!" She knew nothing about the brother—her husband had always been vague in his references to him—and it was only now that she learned what had happened.

His brother had murdered his wife, many years before, and had been tried, convicted, and sentenced to hang. When the sentence of the court had been pronounced, her husband had gone to see his brother who had told him he was not afraid, that he knew he would have to die. He was only worried about him but he should not grieve. He would return.

And so he seems to have done.

The boy says he remembers the gallows, and how he felt as the trap was sprung. After that he forgot everything until, two years old and by then able to express himself, he realized that he had been reborn as his brother's son.

And there is the little Ceylonese girl who, when less than three years old, began talking about her former life. The child started telling her mother about the house where she had lived before, about the post office where her father (her other father) had worked, a mountain she had climbed, and of how she had seen Queen Elizabeth when she toured Ceylon. It appeared that she had been the son of a Ceylonese post office employee, who had died when he was almost fourteen years old.

The two towns were only twenty miles apart, but the girl had never been to the other town and her parents had never known the family of the dead boy. Until that moment.

Investigators confronted her with the boy's mother, under conditions which should have confused her. She recognized the woman immediately and similarly identified her brothers and sisters, in her former life, to the extent of calling them by their pet names. The details of the visit of the Queen, incidents that had happened to the boy in childhood and at school, even the story of the mountain climb—all proved accurate. The little girl, in the opinion of the investigators, had obviously lived and died in the other town, but as a boy, only a few years earlier.

There is the story of the four-year-old boy who returned to the Indian village where he had died, accompanied by his widow.

The boy had kept talking about how his name was so and so, that he belonged to such and such a village, and that he had a wife, three brothers, a mother and a daughter. His grandfather, a minor landowner to judge by the name, visited the village and found that, yes, a man by that name had lived there and had died from the fever, leaving a wife and daughter, the same year the boy had been born. The grandfather sought out the man's family and told them how his grandson kept insisting he was this other man, and a few days later a brother of the dead man made the trip to see for himself what it was all about.

When the boy saw the man and his companion he started

to weep and, without a moment's hesitation, identified his "brother". As the visitors were about to return to their village he grabbed at the man's arm, pleading with him to take him home, and it was only when the grandfather agreed to take the boy there that he became quiet.

The widow and a sister-in-law next visited the boy and were recognized. She arranged to be alone with the boy and asked him to describe some specific event in their married life that would prove to her that he really was her husband reborn. The four year old, after telling her how on one occasion he'd beaten her so hard so that he'd cut her arm, proceeded to tell her details of their marital relations, so intimate and so convincing that she asked that the boy be allowed to return with her to the village. And so the widow and the four-year-old reincarnation of her husband set out on the forty-mile-long return to "their" village.

Before he left, the boy had met his former family, his old friends, and had identified correctly all his former possessions, his will, his garden, four bullocks and two buffalo. On a later visit he met his former daughter, and was so delighted at seeing her again that he wouldn't leave her side and refused to eat unless she was present. There was no apparent explanation for what had happened, beyond the reality that a four-year-old boy, living forty miles from another village (a formidable distance, to put it mildly) had been proven to know everything he might indeed have known if he *had* lived and died in that village.

There was the case of the three-and-a-half-year-old boy, also in India, who came out of a coma that had lasted for several weeks—it had been thought at one moment that he had died—completely altered in character! He was not only not the man's son any longer, he was not even a Jat, he was a Brahmin, a member of a higher caste, and he obviously could not eat the food the others ate. To do so would have been a sin!

A Brahmin neighbor heard of the family's problem and cooked for the boy, using foodstuffs supplied by the family, during the next two years. Unknown to him though, the boy was also eating food from his father's table, and when he discovered the trick played on him, as he viewed it, he was furious. He wanted nothing to do with any of them.

They pointed out though that he had already violated the taboos and eaten the food of a lower caste. Whether he had done so consciously or unconsciously was unimportant. He had done it. And so the boy was talked into giving up, at least temporarily, his rigid Brahmin dietary habits, and he resumed taking his meals with them.

He did not give up his insistence however that he was this other person, a young man from another village, who had been given some poisoned sweets by a man to whom he'd lent money in the past and who had chosen this reliable method of settling the debt.

The boy's family wanted no notoriety about what they regarded as the child's obsession, but it so happened that an acquaintance of the deceased young man, a Brahmin lady, heard about it and traveled, with members of his family, to where the boy lived. They knew that the young man had died as the result of an accident. They knew nothing of the poisoning and were understandably eager to learn more about it.

The child recognized each member of the family, was particularly affectionate to "his" son, and told his interviewers detail after detail of his former life. When he finally did visit the village in which he had lived before his death, he was extremely happy. When he was back home with his lower caste family, the child seemed lonely and unhappy. That was not his home, he protested. It was not his family.

There is the Thai army sergeant who claims to be his uncle, reborn.

When he was four years old he told his parents what his name was and that he was his father's brother reborn.

He told, presumably somewhat later, how he had been killed. He could see his body lying on the ground, the blood rushing from the knife wound. He had wanted to go back to it, but he had been afraid that they would try to kill him again.

He did not return to his body. Instead, still in his spirit form, he visited friends and relatives, increasingly distressed when they too could neither see him nor feel his hands when he would touch him. When he came to his brother's house, he found him at breakfast with his pregnant wife and, as he puts it, he was overcome by a compulsion to enter her body. Which he did. He dwelled there for a few months until it was time for her child to be born, at which time he emerged from her womb, where he had taken "refuge", as his own nephew.

The child identified things that had belonged to the slain man, and proved thoroughly and disturbingly familiar with details of the man's home life, presenting the widow with something of a problem. She was obviously not a married woman, for her husband had been killed, and yet she could hardly consider herself a widow because of the overwhelming evidence that her husband had been reborn in the person of her nephew.

The solution? She became a Buddhist nun.

There is the classic story of a Wisconsin girl who, in the late 1870's, began to have constantly recurring seizures, sometimes several in a day, at times becoming violent, at other times lapsing into unconsciousness. She'd lie still, almost corpselike.

The trances, extending over a period of some six months, had varied effects on the young girl. Sometimes she would obviously experience pain and agony, on other occasions she'd seem to approach ecstacy. As other young girls have done at various times in the last four or five hundred years, she would speak of heaven and of the angels and of how she had talked to the dead.

In other countries or even areas there might have been different reactions. Here a man whose young daughter had died after suffering similar fits, and a friend of his, a physician and a prominent psychical researcher, became interested in the case. When the two arrived at the girl's home, they found her in a trance sitting by the stove. At the moment she claimed to be an elderly woman, then someone else, likewise dead, would take her over. Concerned over the constant changes, they suggested to her that the spirits that controlled her might perhaps send someone a shade more intelligent. The girl proceeded to name a number of people, all dead, who were quite willing to come, and then broke off saying that there was one whom the angels had chosen—the man's daughter.

When she woke up the next morning she recognized nobody in the family. She was that other girl. She was that man's daughter, and when his wife and daughter came to the home, shortly afterwards, she embraced them and called the young girl by a pet name only the dead girl had used. The child was obviously homesick for her former home so she was finally allowed to go there and for some months she lived with the other family, happy to have returned "home."

Three months later the girl told her "mother" that the other girl was coming back, she closed her eyes as if being led into a trance-like state, and the change took place. When the other girl's personality emerged, she looked around and asked where she was. The woman whom only hours earlier she had called mother told her and she asked to be taken to her home but, within minutes, the old personality was gone and she was once more the returned daughter-of-the-house.

As time passed the personalities occasionally attempted to alternate, the dominance of the one girl receding to allow the personality of the girl in whose body she was dwelling to come to the forefront. Then one day she became very distressed. The other girl was definitely coming back, and she immediately set about getting ready to leave, saying goodby to friends and relatives.

On the appointed day she and her "father" were on their way back to the other house when the transformation took place and on arriving back home the girl not only recognized all the members of her family but seemed to show no ill effects from her experience.

Here was of course a case of possession. The dead girl had temporarily returned in the other girl's body and she would speak of her as a separate and distinctly different personality.

Apart from the fact that there was at no time an attempt to claim that the living was an incarnation of the dead—it was a simple case of temporary possession—the whole method of communication was dramatically different. At no time, when the subject under hypnosis, self-induced or otherwise, is recalling a past life, does another personality claim to be utilizing the body as a means of communication.

Instances of possession such as these are numerous and not always so intelligently and sympathetically coped with as this case was, ninety odd years ago. The case is cited here only by way of underlining the reality that the subject itself, beginning with the Thai army sergeant who, as a disembodied spirit, had this compulsion to enter the body of his pregnant sister-in-law, is infinitely more complex than a relatively cursory study such as this can possibly indicate.

IN CLOSING. . . .

I have said that there is no easy road to Understanding.

I say so again. It should, after all, be obvious that this is so, and that you normally cannot turn aside for a moment from the distractions familiar to our days, assume the lotus pose, and instantly find yourself, for the moments you allot to this, "in contact with the Infinite."

You may convince yourself—you may indeed hypnotize yourself into believing that this indeed is happening to you—but this isn't so. In any faith it is close to blasphemy for the metaphysically untrained to attempt this, or to even think of attempting it! It is not impossible—indeed it has happened often, over the millennia, in Islam and in Christianity and in other faiths, for the man of faith to see visions and to believe himself in communion with God as he has always known Him to be. Religious ecstasy, whether hypnotically or otherwise induced, whether born out of self-mortification or self-deception, is however not the same thing as that experience, vouchsafed only the few, not the fee-paying many, who've studied, not for minutes or for hours but for years, that this might happen.

Principal References

R P Anuruddha—An Introduction into Lamaism — 1959 Hoshiarpur, Vishveshvaran-and Vedic Research Institute

Sri Aurobindo—The Problem of Rebirth — 1952 Pondicherry, Sri Aurobindo Ashram

Morey Bernstein—The Search for Bridey Murphy — 1956 New York, Doubleday

Annie Besant—Reincarnation — 1963 Adyar, Theosophical Publishing House

Ananda Coomaraswamy — Recollection, Indian and Platonic, and On the One and Only Transmigrant — 1944 Baltimore, American Oriental Society

Charles Diehl—Byzantine Empresses — 1963 New York, Knopf

Samuel Dill—Roman Society in the Last Century of the Western Empire — 1962 New York, World

Jean Doresse—The Secret Books of the Egyptian Gnostics — 1960 New York, Viking

Eugenio Garin—Italian Humanism: Philosophy and Civic Life in the Renaissance — 1966 New York, Harper & Row

Manly Palmer Hall—Masonic, Hermetic, Quabbalistic and Rosicrucian Symbolical Philosophy — 1936 Los Angeles, Philosophical Research Society

Manly Palmer Hall—The Judgment of the Soul and the Mystery of Coming Forth By Day — 1935 Los Angeles, Manly Hall Publications

Joseph Head and S L Cranston—Reincarnation: an East-West Anthology — 1968 Wheaton, Theosophical Publishing House

Dr. Milton V. Kline—A Scientific Report on the Search for Bridey Murphy — 1956 New York, Julian Press

C. W. Leadbeater—Life After Death — 1918 Krotona, Theosophical Pub. House

Maulavi S. A. Q. Husaini—Ibn al 'Arabi: The Great Muslim Mystic and Thinker — n.d. Lahore, Ashraf

Muhammed Iqbal—The Development of Metaphysics in Persia — n.d. Lahore, Bazm-i-Iqbal

Denys Kelsey and Joan Grant—Many Lifetimes — 1968 New York, Pocket Books

Noel Langley—Edgar Cayce on Reincarnation — 1968 New York, Paperback Library

Jack Lindsay—Song of a Falling World: Culture during the Break-up of the Roman Empire — 1948 London, Dakers

Erwin Rohde—Psyche: The Cult of Souls and the Belief in Immortality among the Greeks — 1966 New York, Harper & Row

Bertrand Russell—A History of Western Philosophy — 1945 New York, Simon & Schuster

Brad Steiger—We Have Lived Before — 1967 New York, Ace

Jean Steinmann—Saint Jerome and his Times — 1959 Notre Dame, Fides

Janet and James Todd—Voices from the Past — 1960 London, Arrow

Paul Vignaux—Philosophy in the Middle Ages — 1939 London, Burns & Oates

Pedro McGregor—Jesus of the Spirits — 1967 New York, Stein & Day

Name ....

Address ....

Titles required ....

....

- -

The publishers hope that you enjoyed this book and invite you to write for the full list of Tandem titles which is available free of charge.

If you find any difficulty in obtaining these books from your usual retailer we shall be pleased to supply the titles of your choice — packing and postage 9d — upon receipt of your remittance.

WRITE NOW TO:
Universal-Tandem Publishing Co. Ltd.,
14 Gloucester Road,
London SW7

Non-fiction

Science Fiction

U.F.O.s

Occult

Horror

Westerns

The Witchfinders

Ralph Comer

Savage seventeenth-century practices of witch-hunting and burning still have an uncanny effect—300 years later—on an entire village. The whole countryside, dominated by the mysterious Winchmere Hall, retains an atmosphere of powerful evil.

When Robert Lawson, a photographic journalist, comes to Winchmere Hall, he is there to produce an article for a newspaper. But the occult forces of the past draw him into the vortex of a terrifying investigation which builds to a totally unexpected climax.

3/6

The Mirror of Dionysos

Ralph Comer

Over a pint in a City pub Robert Lawson heard a tale of a strange obsession, of a recurrent nightmare, and a haunting, overpowering sense of mortal danger. But of course there had to be a natural explanation, despite the curious behaviour of the beautiful blonde girl who took such an interest in Harry Eagar's affairs.

Even Matthew Cullender, specialist in the supernatural and Lawson's companion in the terrifying adventure at Winchmere Hall, was unconcerned, until the dreams became a hideous reality beyond the boundaries of everyday existence. Then not even Cullender's powerful allies from the occult world could save Lawson from involvement in the struggle between true witchcraft and the evils of diabolism.

4/-

TANDEM MEDICAL

Do Something About Your Health—Michael P Winstanley MRCP, LRCP, MP

Do Something About That Migraine—K M Hay MBE MD MRCGP

Do Something About Those Nerves—R A B Rorie MD DPM

Do Something About Those Arteries—H T N Sears MD MRCP

Do Something About That Rheumatism—J L Struthers MB BChir

All at 5s.

These 'Do Something . . .' books have been written by very able and experienced family doctors, each with a special interest in the subject of his choice. He describes, he explains, he anticipates your questions and gives his answer in a simple straightforward language. It is as though, by some miracle, your own doctor had an hour to spare for conversation with you, and you will, of course, need his advice whenever you are in doubt or difficulty. But it is most important to realize that, when these doubts and difficulties have been discussed with him, you can still do a great deal yourself to overcome them or to learn to live with them.

Whether it is migraine or rheumatism, an emotional trouble or something amiss in the circulation, one of these books will tell you exactly how to make the best of things.

G F Abercrombie VRD MD

General Editor